To my friends, Marlin and
Dessa Kuykendal
Pleasant reading & good fortune.
Lee G. McWorkman
10-22-89

# OILFIELD. DOC

### BY
### LEE G. "BULL PLUG"
### McWORKMAN

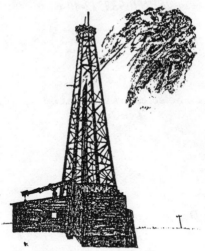

*Sketch of Hendricks No. 1, discovery well in the Wink oil field July 19, 1926*

**PIONEER BOOK PUBLISHERS**
Box 426, Seagraves, Texas 79359

*ISBN 0-933512-40-6*

*Selected art sketches by*
*Lyn Jones*

*Designed by Neil C. Vanzant*

*Produced by*
*PIONEER BOOK PUBLISHERS*
*Box 426, Seagraves, Texas 79359*

# FOREWORD

This book is about the oil field as seen through the eyes of an oil field supply man, from 1946 to the present day, in Texas, New Mexico and the Appalachian areas of Ohio, West Virginia and Pennsylvania. There is nothing magic about the year 1946. It is simply the year in which I came to West Texas and the oil fields. Therefore, I feel that I should be forgiven if I dip into the past prior to that year when the occasion arises.

About the title. A little over a year ago I purchased a computer with word processing, for the purpose of editing this and some others of my manuscripts. These manuscripts and some other items that I need to refer to from time to time are stored in a 20MG hard card in the computer processing unit. To identify the various items stored there it is necessary that each of them have a directory or file name. These names have a maximum length of eight characters each, followed by a period, which in turn is usually followed by the three letters ''doc'', which means document, thusly: Oilfield.doc, meaning simply, oilfield document. After thinking about it for a while I decided that it would make as good a title as any for this book.

[*continued*]

About the cover sketch. While it predates my arrival in West Texas by almost twenty years, I think nothing better symbolizes Winkler County, nor the oil field itself, for that matter, than the Hendrick No. 1 well near Wink. That well was brought in as a producer on July 19, 1926. That well was to change the history of Winkler County. This furnished courtesy of Bill Beckham and *The Winkler County News*.

This is not basically a technical book, and if at times I may make comment or opinions along that line, I would want to emphasize that there is no pretense that they are professional. Nor is it intended as a historical presentation. It reflects a viewpoint, but it is as realistic and factual as I could make it. Included are a number of personal experiences and observations and some of them concern people I have known. In this connection, in those instances where there is the remotest likelihood of personal embarrassment to those involved, the names of individuals or companies are omitted or fictitious ones substituted.

This book is dedicated to the many friends I have made while working and living in the "oil patch".

There are several people who have had a great impact on me in the years I have been in the oil field. Brother Holt, who induced me to join him in this exciting industry and who helped me a great deal in learning about the profession of selling. It was he who introduced me to H.L. (Jelly) Ellis, who gave me a job in the "oil patch" and who also taught me much and exerted a great influence on me. Then there was Jack Miller who was Assistant District Manager under Jelly Ellis with Republic Supply Company. He had a keen mind and I learned much from him. When I once said to him: "You can't make people buy from you", he replied: "No, but you can make them want to!" And there was Rudy Holman, undoubtedly one of the best salesmen I ever knew. Several customers told me: "I don't know why, but when I get ready to buy something, I think about old Rudy". All of these fine gentlemen have gone to their just reward, but I shall certainly never forget them.

iv

"We are all a part of all that we have ever met". Surely these men and some other beautiful people I have had the privilege of knowing since 1946 have had much to do with whatever success I may have had. God bless them all.

While it is hoped that the financial rewards of publishing this book will at least reimburse me for my expenditures, the experience of putting this book together has been rewarding in itself. The search for additional information on certain portions of the book, the quest for some photos that are almost collector's items in themselves, the taking of some snapshots myself, these have at times made me feel like a detective of sorts. I wish to express my gratitude to the many friends who have helped me in this respect. Throughout the book itself I have, from time to time, made specific acknowledgements of these contributions.

It is hoped that this book will be a source of entertainment to my many friends and others in the oil patch. But I also hope that it will somehow convey a message to those others in our great country who are less informed on the oil and gas industries, to the end that they will have a better understanding of their problems.

# CONTENTS

| CHAPTER | TITLE | PAGES |
|---|---|---|
| I | THE EARLY YEARS | 1 |
| II | THE TOOLPUSHER | 6 |
| III | SANDSTORMS AND BLUE NORTHERS | 13 |
| IV | WINK | 16 |
| V | THE MID-CONTINENT SUPPLY COMPANY SIGN | 24 |
| VI | ENTER THE WATERFLOOD | 27 |
| VII | THE HENDRICKS REEF | 30 |
| VIII | MENTONE AND LOVING COUNTY | 32 |
| IX | MESQUITE BUSHES AND SOME OTHER THINGS | 34 |
| X | A MISUNDERSTOOD INDUSTRY | 39 |
| XI | THE TRAINS AND THE WINDMILLS | 45 |
| XII | A MEMORABLE NEW YEAR'S DAY | 47 |
| XIII | A TODDY FOR THE BODY | 49 |
| XIV | THE LAND OF ENCHANTMENT | 51 |
| XV | ROLL AND WHISTLE | 52 |
| XVI | HOBBS, NEW MEXICO | 54 |
| XVII | THE LUNCHEON | 56 |
| XVIII | GETTING STUCK IN THE MUD AT ROSWELL | 57 |
| XIX | THE GRAND OPENING | 58 |
| XX | SLEEPING IN THE BRADY HOTEL | 60 |
| XXI | TO ELECTRIFY A LEASE | 61 |
| XXII | BACK TO KERMIT | 63 |
| XXIII | THE AGE OF THE MINISKIRT | 65 |
| XXIV | RUSSIAN ROULETTE | 67 |

| | | |
|---|---|---|
| XXV | A CROWDED STORE | 68 |
| XXVI | THE MARK OF A PRO | 69 |
| XXVII | THE STUCK PUMP | 71 |
| XXVIII | THE NIPPLE CHASERS | 72 |
| XXIX | PECK WILLIAMS AND DOCTOR DUNN | 76 |
| XXX | LARCENY IN THE OIL FIELD | 78 |
| XXXI | ANOTHER FORM OF LARCENY, THE DESIGN SUB-SURFACE PUMP | 79 |
| XXXII | THE STORE MANAGER'S SCHOOL | 81 |
| XXXIII | A MATTER OF OPINION | 84 |
| XXXIV | A TEXAN GOES TO OHIO | 85 |
| XXXV | A LAND OF PROMOTERS | 88 |
| XXXVI | THE CAPTAIN ON THE BRIDGE | 90 |
| XXXVII | A DIFFERENT TERRAIN | 91 |
| XXXVIII | THE BIG INTERCHANGE | 92 |
| XXXIX | THE PIPE CRUNCH | 93 |
| XL | THE GOOF-UP | 96 |
| XLI | THE OHIO OIL AND GAS ASSOCIATION MEETING | 97 |
| XLII | BUCKEYE SUPPLY COMPANY | 98 |
| XLIII | EARLY RETIREMENT AND BACK TO KERMIT | 99 |
| XLIV | THE BOOM | 103 |
| XLV | THE BUST AND THE AFTERSHOCKS | 106 |
| XLVI | A MATTER OF ECONOMICS AND NATIONAL SECURITY | 111 |
| XLVII | A CHANGE OF SCHEDULE | 116 |
| XLVIII | OUT OF TOWN SELLING | 117 |
| XLIX | SOME OIL FIELD NICKNAMES | 121 |
| L | PUTTING THINGS IN PERSPECTIVE | 122 |

[*continued*]

| LI | AN OFFICE TO REMEMBER | 123 |
|---|---|---|
| LII | TO STIMULATE A WELL | 126 |
| LIII | SELLING BY TELEPHONE REACHING OUT | 127 |
| LIV | PRANKS IN A SUPPLY STORE | 128 |
| LV | NOT A MATTER OF SAVING MONEY | 130 |
| LVI | DE-JA VU AND NOSTALGIA | 131 |
| LVII | THE PERMIAN PETROLEUM EXPOSITION IN ODESSA,TEXAS | 132 |
| LVIII | THE WINK SINK | 136 |
| LIX | NO NUMBER THIRTEEN | 138 |
| LX | NOT ON PRICE ALONE | 140 |
| LXI | TRADEMARKS | 141 |
| LXII | NOT STARVING TO DEATH | 142 |
| LXIII | SOME UNEXPECTED CHANGES | 143 |
| LXIV | ESPRIT DE CORPS | 144 |
| LXV | "BULL DOG" | 147 |
| LXVI | THE ROLE OF THE OIL FIELD SUPPLY COMPANY IN THE INDUSTRY | 151 |
| LXVII | A SALES MEETING TO REMEMBER | 154 |
| LXVIII | AND NOW, 1987 | 156 |
| LXIX | THE RANCHERS | 158 |
| LXX | THE CAPS | 161 |
| LXXI | THE PEOPLE WHO HAD THE COURAGE TO TRY | 164 |
| LXXII | AND NOW THE STOCK MARKET PLUNGE | 165 |
| LXXIII | ANOTHER SCAM; THE LIMITED PARTNERSHIP DRILLING FUND | 166 |
| LXXIV | THE LAST TIME AROUND | 169 |
| LXXV | THE DEATH OF A COMPANY | 171 |

# Chapter I

## THE EARLY YEARS

It was in the mid-twenties. A lady was talking. "I don't like to see my boys going to work in those rough old oil fields. The people in the oil field are different - there's a lot of drinking and other things going on in the oil fields."

It was Mama talking. Older brother, Holt, had gone to the oil fields in the vicinity of Seminole, Oklahoma a year before. He had gone to work for the old Gypsy Oil company, later to become Gulf Oil Corporation. Brother Doug, two and a half years younger than Holt, was getting teady to go now. Doug said: "Now Mama, it isn't all that bad." Mama was far from convinced, but Doug went ahead anyway. The Great Depression was yet to come, but for us it was already here. We were poor Arkansas farmers. Good jobs were hard to find. Doug didn't stay in the oil fields but a year or so, but Holt stayed. He left the Gypsy Company and went into the business of supplying the equipment needs of the oil and gas industry. He would work twenty-six years for The S.M. Jones Company, a firm who had headquarters in Toledo, Ohio, and who manufactured sucker rods. Some of you old-timers in the oilfield may remember that they painted their sucker rods green. And a little over twenty years after he had gone to Seminole I joined him in the "oil patch", as many refer to it, in West Texas, and I have been there ever since. In 1955 Holt left the S.M. Jones Co. and went into business for himself as a manufacturer's representative.

We should clarify right now what it means to be identified with the oil industry. To people unfamiliar with it they think of it in rather limited terms:

Millionare oil barons on the one hand and muddy, sweaty, sometimes uncouth, roughnecks on the other. Many people do not realize just how many mouths are fed by the oil industry and how broad a spectrum of humanity, economically, culturally and intellectually, is involved. To those of you who have been around somewhere in the oilfield for a number of years, as I have been, that which is to follow may be a little boring, but to those of you who have not, it should prove enlightening. And I feel that it must be said. So all of you old hands in the oil patch bear with me for a short time while I enumerate just who all are involved in this exciting industry.

To begin with, there is the landowner who, unless he has sold his mineral rights to someone else, has more than an academic interest in what is found beneath the surface of his property. His interest, known as royalty, varies, but one-eighth is probably the most common, which means that his share of the oil and/or gas production on his property will be one-eighth. Then, of course, there is the oil or gas company, who hopefully for all concerned, will be successful in drilling a producing well. In order to do this they must have landmen, geologists, reservoir engineers, drilling foremen, and people to produce the wells if successful.

Most oil companies contract their drilling to drilling contractors. A typical drilling contractor has a drilling superintendent. Then, on each drilling rig they have at least one toolpusher, three drillers - one for each shift or "Tour" - and twelve or fifteen roughnecks, at least four, more often five, on each Tour. To allow for vacations and days off, most rigs have at least one more drilling crew.

In order to drill and complete a well an army of other people are involved: Dirt contractors, with their bulldozers and other equipment, to prepare the locations, and build the access roads; mud engineers; service companies who cement, perforate, log, fracture and perform other services; trucking contractors who not only move the heavy drilling equipment from one location to another, but haul in the casing and tubing needed to drill and complete the well.

Backing up all of the above are oil field supply company people who expedite getting the materials to the drilling site as needed. Once the well is drilled to total depth — and hopefully production is indicated — a host of other people take over: Oil well servicing and completion units; oil field construction crews laying flow lines, setting oil and gas separators and storage tanks. From the producing lease we enter an entirely new world of gas and oil processing and transportation.

Of course, to make all of this possible and to enable the drilling contractor, the producer, the pipe line companies and the processing plants to do their thing, there is an impressive array of manufacturers especially oriented toward these types of operations.

So the millionaire, with the ten-gallon Stetson hat and the Cadillac has a lot of help doesn't he? And a lot of mouths are fed in the process.

As was the case with Brother Holt, it was in the supply phase of the oil and gas industry that I was associated.

In some respects Mama was right. The "booms" in the earlier years were on the rough and tough side: Seminole, Borger, Wink, Burkburnett, East Texas, even the Snyder, Texas boom in the late 40's and early 50's had some of the color of the earlier ones. But two things should be made clear. For one, the oil field never was, nor it it now, a place for the timid. It takes

3

*The Old Republic Supply Company Store in Odessa, Texas*
[*Circa 1948*]

people of guts to survive. Second, it was rough but the oil field has never had the basic evil in it that exists in organized crime. What evil there has been in the oil industry has been incidental to its existence, not contrived. And, of course, there have been a number of cases where the fast buck artist and other undesirable elements of sociey have followed the oil field, particularly the booms. There may be those who would disagree with this premise, but I believe that what I have said is basically correct.

It was January 3, 1946, when I went to work for Republic Supply Company. I had been honorably discharged from the Army Air Corps in November of 1945 and had purposely delayed looking for a job until

4

*H.L. [Jelly] Ellis, District Manager, Republic, West Texas and Southeast New Mexico*

after Christmas and I had been given a chance to visit my Mother and brothers and sisters.

After approximately four and a half years in the military service the "outside" was a rather strange place - it took some time to adjust to it. I started out at Republic's Odessa, Texas store. My job was not a "position". My early orientation included showing me where the broom, the mop and the trash cans were located. I was also shown where the Post Office and the bank were located, to which I walked, not drove.

## Chapter II

## THE TOOLPUSHER

In those days it was common practice for the supply store salesmen and the toolpushers and drilling superintendents to stand around the counter in a supply store and play pitch or poker and not at all unusual for them to take a "nip" from a whiskey bottle from time to time...I am not talking about after hours. This went on in the morning and for hours at a time. Then one or the other of the men would say he had to get out to the rig or rigs and the game was over.

Also, at that point in time it was not too unusual for a toolpusher to have two or more rigs to see after. He was a pretty busy man, particularly when one or more of the rigs was rigging up, setting pipe or on a fishing job. When there were problems on a rig, the toolpusher frequently would sleep in the back seat of his car with instructions left with the driller to wake him up if anything happened that he should know about. It was not until much later that a toolpusher was assigned to one rig only, indeed, when on large rigs drilling deep wells, several toolpushers would be assigned to a rig and work in shifts. Also somewhat later, trailer houses were provided for toolpushers to stay in.

On many rigs at that time the toolpusher had to be a pretty rough and ready type of man for it was expected that he could hold his own against any of the men under his supervision. Another frequent custom at that time was for roughnecks to stay with their driller. If he quit, they quit. By the same token, if he was fired, they were probably fired, too, as the driller who replaced him would have his own men. On some rigs the drillers stayed with the toolpusher in the same way, and in those instances all of the men working on a rig might

6

leave at one time. A seven day week was common in those days, also vacations for drillers and roughnecks were practically unheard of.

A rookie oil field supply man was considered fair game for the men on a rotary drilling rig. On his first visit to the rig his initiation into the fraternity often took the form of his being thrown into the mud pit or having the rear wheels of his car jacked up when he wasn't looking. And of course, they would order striped paint and sky hooks from him.

Most of the toolpushers were reasonable people and tried to make it as easy as possible on the supply man, but mixed in with these nice guys were some who seemed to delight in causing extra work for us.

I recall one instance in particular, when a toolpusher came by our store and asked me to deliver a case of light bulbs to his rig. When he left the store I supposed he was on his way to his house or possibly to his company's office. But out on the dirt road to the rig I followed a trail of dust. You guessed it! It was the toolpusher. He had caused me to make a completely unnecessary trip.

On Saturday mornings when I called on drilling rigs, I would check with the daylight driller or toolpusher to be sure that they had enough of the commonly used expendable items, like lightbulbs, drill pipe dope, tong dies, and spinning rope, to last them through the weekend. On the occasion at hand, the daylight driller had asked me to tell the toolpusher that they needed some lightbulbs, tong ties and some spinning rope, too, as they would be running casing during the weekend. When I talked to the toolpusher about this he gave me a hard time and told me that if I dared to bring any of the aforementioned material to the rig that he would cut me off from selling them anything in the future. So I left

7

the rig. But at 9:00 Sunday morning the phone rang. It was the toolpusher. He ordered the very same items that we had discussed the previous morning. And hurry! He needed the stuff right away.

One of the bigger problems facing drilling contractors was - and still is - when they had fishing jobs: drill pipe twisted off; cones broken off the rock bits; stuck drill collars. Some drillers and toolpushers were better fishermen than others. Experience most certainly played a part in this but some of them just seemed to have a gift for "seeing", visualizing if you prefer, what it looked like down there where the fish was located and could select the right fishing tool and had that right touch for getting the fish. This ability as a "fisherman" is a valuable talent, as fishing jobs have been known to last for days, even weeks, and on the deeper wells the cost can easily run into six figures.

Besides fishing jobs there are other things that haunt the drilling contractor: crooked holes; blowouts and lost circulaton. The last two named sometimes come as a twin threat. That is, in some zones, in trying to keep the mud weight up in order to prevent a well from blowing out, there is a danger of breaking down the formation and losing circulation. Under those circumstances the people affected are sort of "between a rock and a hard place." Those involved draw a big sigh of relief when casing is finally set through the culprit zone. As in the case of fishing jobs, the above problems can become quite expensive.

Oil Field Supply stores almost always had living quarters for at least part of their personnel. This would be in the form of a bunkhouse in the store building itself or in a house nearby. This custom not only provided housing for the employees, which wasn't always readily available otherwise, but also assured ready personnel to take care of customers emergency needs at any time of the day or night, Sundays and Holidays included.

Drinking in the bunkhouse was not unusual, nor were poker games. Customers frequently joined the supply men in both activities.

During this era, a time card meant very little to a supply man. The standard work week was fifty-four hours - nine hours a day, six days a week. But he was supposed to work whenever he was needed. If things weren't too busy, if he goofed off some, that was alright, too.

There were quite a few steam-powered rotary drilling rigs still running in West Texas in 1946. A lot of arguments took place between the old dyed-in-the-wool steam rig men and their counter-parts who were exponents of the relatively new power rigs. Steam undoubtedly was a good source of power - positive power at any speed, and it was its own torque converter - but its greater weight and bulk, plus the need for large quantities of water, which in West Texas is sometimes hard to come by - assured that the days of the steam rig were numbered. But it was sure a good place for drillers and roughnecks to launder their greasy clothes and the boilerman could cook some awfully good steaks.

In 1946 there were approximately forty rotary drilling rigs running in the Keystone Field of Winkler County, a field lying roughly seven miles northeast of the City of Kermit. Drilling was to several pays and depths: The Devonian (8,000 feet, approx.), The Silurian (8,500 to 9,000), and Ellenberger (10,000 and deeper). There were also some wells drilled to the Holt (4,800 to 5,000 feet) Earlier there had been wells in the Keystone Colby, at a depth of 2,800 to 3,000 feet. And I think there are some other, intermediate pays that I have overlooked.

The drilling contractors in the Keystone Field at that point in time as I can best remember were Richardson and Bass (they had five or six rigs, I believe, some power, some steam). Dillard and Waltermire, McDaniel and Beecherl, Big West Drilling company, McQueen and Clevenger, Sharp Drilling Company,, Norwood Drilling company, Gardner Brothers Drilling Company and I am sure I have overlooked some. Surely there was a George P. Livermore or a Loflin rig around there somewhere!

In 1946, an oil well drilled to a depth of ten thousand feet was considered a deep one. Two miles into the earth seemed awfully deep in those days. A depth of thirty thousand feet really would have seemed deep. But it should be borne in mind that at the time we are talking about, ten or eleven thousand feet was about as deep as the existing equipment was designed for. It is a great credit to the various segments of the manufacturing and service companies serving the oil and gas industries, that they kept pace with the needs of deeper drilling as they arose. On the drilling rig itself this involved heavier derricks, crown blocks, traveling blocks, swivels, hooks, elevators, tongs and of course draw-works and power units to correspond with the increased loads. Also, there was a need for larger diameter, stronger hoisting lines and the greater depths demanded mud pumps that could provide higher mud pressures in larger volumes. It should be mentioned also that the manufacturers of drilling mud and of rock bits kept up with the increasing demands of deeper drilling.

The deeper wells also presented a challenge to the manufacturers of drill pipe, casing and tubing. It

10

should be observed in passing that the design of a string of casing must meet three often conflicting basic requirements: tensile strength, internal pressure strength and resistance to collapse. I say conflicting in that by increasing the weight of the casing in the lower portion of the string in order to resist collapse from the hydrostatic load of deep formations, you are also increasing the tensile load on the upper part of the string. In designing these strings it is preferred that a nice safety factor be maintained. It can be seen that on a very deep string it is hard to design one that will do the job and have an adequate safety factor as well. It is a great credit to the pipe manufacturers that they have met this challenge so well. It should be stated also that there has been a fine degree and spirit of cooperation between manufacturers, service organizations, oil operators and drilling contractors in meeting the needs and problems of deeper drilling. This in spite of a governmental climate that indeed at times seemed almost designed to discourage progress in the industry.

The value of natural gas was not as fully appreciated then as it is today and much of it was burned in flares. Many fields were so lit up by these flares that a newspaper could be read by their light on a dark night. But the Texas Railroad Commission shortly brought this practice to a halt. Not only was energy being wasted, if not otherwise used this gas needed to be reinjected into the producing formation to maintain field gas pressure.

In 1946 there was quite a bit of gas in the atmosphere, too. At Kermit, Texas, anything colored blue was affected by this gas - automobiles, clothes, whatever - over a period of time they would take on a shade that was a mixture of the primary colors. Fortunately, this gas was not dangerous, although sometimes I had headaches that I suspected were caused by the gas. In some areas of West Texas, however, the natural gas was deadly. This was particularly true of that in the McElroy Field in Crane and Upton Counties, which had a high percentage of hydrogen sulphide.

While I started out with Republic Supply Company at their Odessa, Texas store, after a few months I was transferred to their Monahans store. Then, after being there about two weeks, I was transferred to the Kermit store. As in the other two stores I lived in the company bunkhouse there.

There were quite a few old Superior two-cycle gas engines on pumping wells in those days. They would be the last thing I would hear when I went to sleep at night and the first thing I heard when I woke in the morning. There were still some central powers operating; one big engine pumping a number of wells by means of rod lines extending radially from the engine to the individual wells. Some of these engines, like the Lorain and Weber, are no longer manufactured.

In 1946, West Texas was still new country. With the exception of a few pioneer ranch families and a few others, almost anyone you met was a first generation West Texan, or at the very most, second generation. They had come to West Texas from West Central Texas, from Kansas, Oklahoma, Arkansas, East Texas or somewhere else, but almost certainly did not grow up in our area. We were the advance cadre—we felt a certain kindred pioneering spirit and closeness.

The few that were already here were fine people; the Mitchells, the Campbells, the Bairds, the Waltons, the Eddins, the Summers, the Whittens, the Lineberrys, the Burrows, the Williams, the Haleys and the Tarvers. And I know that I have missed some people and for this oversight I beg their forgiveness.

12

# Chapter III

## SANDSTORMS AND BLUE NORTHERS

In the late 1940's there were a lot of sand and dust storms in the spring months. During this time you could almost bet that by 2:00 in the afternoon the sky would be a yellowish pink and the wind would be blowing the stuff. The sand and/or dust would blow at velocities of from fifteen to forty or fifty miles per hour until approximately 7:00 in the eveining. This would happen day after day during the spring. Many times it would be necessary to use headlights on automobiles during the day. Sometimes it would blow all day and all night, too. There just wasn't any way you could keep from getting some of the sand and dirt into your house. Small wonder that some young wives from Ohio or other green areas of the country were disenchanted with West Texas! One time - I believe this was in the 50's - the sand and dust blew night and day for a solid week.

For some reason we do not now have the sandstorms that we had in those days. In this connection, it is a fact not necessarily universally known, that the so-called sand hills in this area are not the source of the sand of the sandstorms we have had here. The sand in the hills area is too heavy to be airborne - it will creep along the ground and drift, but will not blow up into the air to any height. The sand and dust in the sandstorms we have here actually comes from northern New Mexico and Colorado. I have seen these storms rolling in like the tide - I have also seen them pass through our area like express trains.

One Saturday afternoon when I was living in Hobbs, New Mexico, I made a delivery of some material to a

13

drilling rig about fifteen miles west of Tatum. It was one of the big rigs, with a high sub-structure, and from the derrick floor you could see quite a distance. As I chatted with the driller, I looked across the prairie to the north. At a distance of six to eight miles one of those sandstorms was rolling in like the waves on a seashore. I told the driller that, unless he needed me for something else, I believed I would head for Hobbs and maybe get there before the sandstorm did. I would estimate that I averaged sixty miles an hour in driving to Hobbs. About fifteen minutes after I got there the storm hit. I figure that it had to be moving south at a speed of at least fifty miles an hour!

In the earlier years we also had quite a few "Blue Northers." The best way I can describe them is that the clouds in the northern sky took on a deep blue hue (hence the name) and in a matter of a very short time there was a dramatic change in temperature in a downward direction. We might be standing outside in our shirt sleeves at one point in time and twenty minutes later shivering and looking for an overcoat.

I especially remember one Blue Norther. In 1950, Kermit had a very good football team. They made it to the state playoffs, being defeated by Wharton in the final game. I was living in Hobbs, New Mexico, at the time but I pretty well kept up with the Kermit team. Jack Miller and I went to Odessa and watched them play Littlefield in the bi-district game. As I remember, Kermit won that game rather easily. But what I remembered most about the game was that late in the third quarter a Blue Norther blew in. Jack and I both had on light sweaters or coats, but they weren't nearly enough. I thought we were going to freeze. After the game we went to a friend's house and had some drinks. These drinks went a long way in thawing us out.

I mentioned earlier that we don't have the sandstorms that we had thirty to forty years ago. Neither do we have the Blue Northers. I think, indeed, that the weather has changed somewhat.

When I came to West Texas in 1946, just about all of the oil and gas companies provided housing for their full-time employees and their families. This was done in the form of "camps" that were located on or near the leases or plants where they were employed. These camps ranged in size from a couple or three houses for an independent oil company to several dozen houses in a major oil company camp. Some of the very large camps had as many as a hundred houses in them. But just about all of these company camps have now been phased out. Many of the houses in these camps were sold to the employees living in them and moved to town.

One of these camps was the Humble (now Exxon) Means Camp, a few miles north of the city of Andrews. After moving the houses out of the camp, the Company donated the campsite, with its many nice trees, to Andrews County to be used as a county park.

Cabot Corporation had a camp next to their gasoline plant northwest of Kermit. The plant foreman and the operators said that they would go to sleep hearing the compressor engines running. If one of the engines stopped running or wasn't running smoothly it would wake them up. And they would even know which one of the engines it was!

## Chapter IV

## WINK

In those days it was ten miles by road to Wink - it is now only eight miles, as a new, shorter road was built around 1950. Wink had its boom in the late twenties and early thirties. I was not there - Brother Holt went there from time to time - but from all reports it was a rip-roaring boom town in true boom tradition. Estimates of the population of Wink during that period vary from twenty to thirty thousand people. I have also been told that from three to four thousand of these people were so-called undesirables. I can only say that the people who stayed in Wink were good people. Through the years I have acquired many good friends in Wink. A number of them have gone to their just reward.

One of my good friends was Mr. R.F. Mackin. Mack managed Lam Tex Equipment Company for many years, then he and his associates purchased the business from the owners in 1961 and operated it as Winkler County Pump and Supply for a number of years. The company sold all kinds of oil field supplies, but specialized in sub-surface pumps, expecially casing pumps. Mack was Mr. Casing Pump himself, for West Texas and New Mexico. But his reputation as a foremost expert in that field extended much further. Men came from foreign countries to share in his expertise. They would come to Wink from Saudi Arabia, Iran and Egypt and perhaps some other countries, at different times, and would be the Mackin's house guests for something like a week while Mack instructed them. In addition to demonstrations in the pump repair shop, he would take them on field

*Mr. R.F. Mackin*

trips. He also lectured at an oil-oriented class at Texas Tech in Lubbock.

During the forty or so years that the business was in operation the doors of the store were never locked. When a customer needed something after hours, on Sundays or on holidays, he simply went in the store, got what he needed and wrote it on a notepad on the office wall. Through the years I doubt that much, if any, material was lost or stolen.

Mack was a pretty good story teller, too. When he related a tale the listener became so involved in the story that he was there and became a part of it. I recall one account that he told about in which he was lost in a snowstorm in a very large wheat field in Kansas. I became so involved in the story that I was actually concerned about his safety. Only after I returned to reality did I know that he was alright.

One of the phenomena of West Texas - a man made one - was the fabulous Wink football team of the 1930's. In their first years, from 1928 to 1936, they played 87 games, of which they won 63, lost 19 and tied 5. They were not picky about who they played, either. They would play just about any team that had the courage to face them. They played both Midland and Odessa, and beat them. I heard one story - unconfirmed - that they even challenged Texas Tech, but that the latter declined with thanks.

A number of my friends played on those teams; the Dodd boys - for years there was always at least one of

First Wink Wildcat Football Team...1929

them on the team - John R. Lee, Orville Youngblood, Beekie Ezelle and his brothers, Charlie Dennis, J.R. Callihan, Johnny Hodgett, John D. Crawford, Ralph Pritchard, Charlie Wight, Bert Page.

While the Wink football team of the 30's attracted the most notoriety, the overall record of the Wink teams to the present day has been pretty good. As of 1984, their teams had played a total of 602 games, winning 385, losing 202, and tying 15, with a 63.95 winning percentage. From the inception of the team in 1928 they had faced 92 different opponents!

While the coaches and players deserve due credit for the outstanding records of the teams through the years, the strong support of the Wink townspeople most certainly has been a contributing factor. That spirit still exists in Wink.

It has been said that on a Friday night during a football game, you could shoot a cannon down Hendricks Boulevard, the main street in Wink, and never harm a soul. Everyone in town would be at the game!

And when the football game was out of town, the people in the town went too. There was an expression around the town that whoever left Wink last to go to the football game would "turn out the lights."

Amazingly, there was very little in the way of thefts durng that period of time. Anyone who would take advantage of the situation would be a very low person, indeed! Besides, just about everybody was at the football game, anyway!

Many of the Wink boys served in the Armed Services, in World War II and some other conflicts. Several of them sustained injuries in these military actions. And some of them never returned.

19

I am indebted to Mrs. O.L. (Krick) Youngblood and to Mr. Martin Hammer for some of the background material on Wink. Krick now resides in Kermit, but grew up in Wink - she was Kristina Cooper then - and was a cheerleader in high school in the 30's. Martin also grew up in Wink and still lives there. He played baritone and was drum major in the Wink Wildcat marching band in the early 40's. He also played football in his last two years in high school. I am also indebted to Mrs. Helen Dunn, one of the late Mr. Mackin's daughters, for some photos and also some pertinent information concerning her father.

In 1946, Midland and Odessa were the two big towns in the area, and as now, the centers of activity for the Permian Basin - Midland for the oil company offices, Odessa for the drilling contractors and supply companies. Midland had a population of 13,000, approx., Odessa 9,500.

The Scharbauer Hotel was the gathering place for oil men in Midland. In Odessa it was the Elliott Hotel and the Frisco Cafe. The night spots in Odessa were Danceland, The Ace of Clubs and the Roski Club.

At that point in time when you drove to the Andrews Highway or the Kermit Highway from downtown Odessa you were pretty well out in the country. The road from Odessa to Kermit was caliche and had some pretty bad places in it. The road from Kermit to Mentone, to the west in Loving county, was even worse and there was a very good chance of getting stuck in the sand when making the trip. It was quite a bit further but the best, and surest, way to go to Mentone or Orla was by way of Pecos.

One of the favorite eating spots of the time was "Ben's" Mexican Food Restaurant in Pecos. It was not at all uncommon for people to drive there from

20

Midland, Odessa and Kermit to eat. I understand that some people still drive that far to eat there.

The road from Kermit to Hobbs, New Mexico - sixty miles to the north - wasn't too good a road either. The worst part of this road was the eighteen mile stretch between Eunice and Hobbs. There were a lot of chuck holes in it and it was nicknamed "suicide lane." There was a lot of traffic on it and dust was continually fogging up over it.

Sometimes we would meet the people at our Hobbs store with material that they needed from our store or the other way around. A place about ten miles north of Jal, New Mexico, on the west side of the highway, known as Bill's Bar was about halfway between Kermit and Hobbs, so that was our meeting spot. They served mixed drinks, beer and sandwiches at Bill's. After we had met, if it was during the day, we might visit over a beer and a sandwich. If it was at night, we might take on several beers when we met.

At that time the population of Kermit was approximately three-thousand. Highway 302 was strictly out in the country. There was no hospital at that time, Robinson's Clinic being the only facility with any beds. As to restaurants there were Master's, Gipps, the Blue Bonnet, Mack's (it was on the Jal Highway at the time) and The Hut, which was on the curve on the Jal Highway just as you left town. There also was the Interurban Inn, a streetcar converted into a cafe and beer joint. Things got pretty lively there at times. For bars there were also Weaver's Down Town Bar and Weaver's Drive In, which was on the curve of the road to Wink, not far from where National Supply Company had their store. Watson's Drive Inn was also nearby. It would be several years later that the Winter garden and the El Morocco would be opened.

21

There was only one bank in Kermit, the Kermit State Bank, and it was located in the southeast corner of the intersection of Austin and Pine streets. It was in a long, narrow building and it seemed crowded, but I suppose it pretty well served the needs of the community at that time. As for myself, my need for a bank at that point in time was not too great, as I spent my pay checks about as fast as I got them.

In those early years it was not at all uncommon for residents of Kermits to have chickens, geese, rabbits, goats or pigs on their premises. In those days hearing a rooster crow in the early morning hours was not an unusual thing. I think there might have even been a few cows and horses, too. But a few years later a City Ordinance was passed forbidding this practice.

Back in those days the coyotes came in pretty close to town, too. And every so often one would be seen in the city limits. No doubt the presence of chickens and rabbits and other small animals had something to do with their attraction to our city.

Housing was scarce in Kermit back in those days. Much of what was available was rather crude and primitive. Quite a few people lived in trailer houses. The age of motels had not arrived but we had several hotels; The Weatherby, the Reneau, the Kermit Hotel, the Austin and the Texhoma. The latter served family style meals. I ate there a number of times. While a few travelers may have stayed in these hotels, most of their occupants were people who worked on drilling rigs or did other oil field work. There were also several rooming houses in Kermit at that point in time.

I am told that, in the earlier years, the late Mr. Sid Richardson stayed in the Texhoma Hotel when he was in Kermit. I never had the pleasure of meeting Mr. Richardson, but I believe that I would have liked him.

22

When I came to Kermit in 1946 he had overcome his financial difficulties and was at the top of the heap. I heard a number of stories about him. In the years when he was struggling some suppliers of materials and services would extend credit to him, but a lot of them would not. Also, in those lean years he was not always able to pay his employees on pay day. But they stayed with him anyway, some for as long as a year, without a paycheck. Of course, when things got better he did pay them. But the significant thing, to me, is that he never forgot the people and companies who stood by him when the going was rough. Surely that is something we should all admire and respect him for.

When I first came to the Kermit store there was a fellow working there who for the most part did paperwork. He was single, too, and we both lived in the bunkhouse. One Saturday night we were nipping away at a jug of whiskey and swapping tales. As was typical of me in those days, the more we drank the richer we became! We then hit upon the brilliant idea of hiring a cab - neither of us had a car - to take us to Hobbs, a distance of sixty miles, to see the bright lights. At a dollar a mile that was sixty dollars - a lot of money in those days. But we went, and returned to Kermit early Sunday morning. But we rode a bus back and barely had enough money for that!

## Chapter V

## THE MID-CONTINENT SUPPLY COMPANY SIGN

Mid-Continent Supply Company's store in Kermit was in the same block as Republic's. Like all their other stores they had an illuminated simulation of an oil field derrick atop their store building. The lights on the derrick changed according to a cycle created by a little motor in the light circuit. We didn't have TV yet, but did have a radio in our bunkhouse. As the Mid-Continent derrick lights went through their phases the radio would squawk. This, of course, was disturbing and we discussed the possibilities of removing the fuse or cutting the wire that furnished electricity to the derrick. Of course, we were never really serious about doing this. But one Saturday afternoon we were all gone except a fellow who reprsented a vendor with whom we did business - the name of the fellow and the vendor shall remain nameless - and who at the time was staying in our bunkhouse. It was near the Christmas holidays and he had a case of pint bottles of Early Times bourbon whiskey that his company had provided him with to distribute among their customers. He had been rather liberally partaking of the bourbon himself. He also had been attempting to listen to a very crucial football game. Of course the Mid-Continent sign would interrupt the game from time to time and seemed to do so at the worst possible times, like when it was fourth down and six inches to go on the one foot line. Our friend's consequent frustration, plus the influence of the bourbon, caused him to decide to do something about it. He found the wire that led to the sign and with the aid of some pliers he proceeded to put the sign out

24

*A Typical Mid-Continent Supply Company of the 1940's. [Note the derrick sign above the store]*

of business. but in doing so, as he described later, the pliers turned blue and for a time he couldn't turn loose from them!

The accompanying photograph is of the old Mid-Continent store at Odessa, Texas, but it is typical of the many stores that company had back at the time the picture was taken. My thanks to Phil Flehmer, manager of their Odessa, Texas store, for making it possible for me to have a copy of this picture.

Getting back to the oil and gas industry. It is worthwhile, I think, to point out that most of the deeper drilling has been done in the quest for large reservoirs of natural gas. When successful, very high pressures have often been encountered. It can be seen that this presented problems for the manufacturers of pipe, valves and fittings in that some of these pressures exceeded the design limits of existing equipment.

Unfortunately, too, some of our good oil and gas production occurs coincidently with certain other undesirable compounds, the most common of which is H2S or hydrogen sulphide. Not only must these compounds be eliminated - by a sweetening process - from the gas and oil, in order for them to be marketable products, but they are devastatingly corrosive to the equipment handling this "sour" gas and oil. A number of methods and materials have been used to combat this corrosion: chemicals, corrosion resistant metals, and internal coatings of pipe, valves and fittings with non-corrosive materials such as plastics and cement. None of these methods come cheaply. Of course, this is just another one of the things that some of our less informed legislators and a whole bunch of our citizenry, particularly in the states that don't produce oil or gas, don't know about the oil and gas industry.

# Chapter VI
## ENTER THE WATERFLOOD

While a number of deeper wells had been drilled in the meantime, many of the older, relatively shallow wells (3,000 foot average) in much of Southeastern New Mexico and West Texas were about to "play out" in the late forties. Some of them had flowed at first, then later put on the pump. But after a few years even the pump had reached its limit. Reservoir engineers knew that most of the oil was still in the formation - estimates ranged from sixty to seventy-five percent - but at that point in time that was about the best that they could do.

While some operators had obtained some additonal production by repressuring the formation with produced gas, secondary recovery at that time was, for the most part, either unknown or unproven. Many of these old wells had been sold for salvage purposes in which the casing above the cement would be cut off or "shot off" by means of a string shot and the casing sold for use in other wells.

Then, in the late forties Forest Oil Company started a pilot water flood project in Ward County, West Texas. In less than two years positive returns had been established. The era of waterflooding had begun in West Texas and Southeast New Mexico! In this connection due credit should be given to the late George Buckles, a brilliant engineer, who did the engineering for the initial pilot project and later, for many other waterflood operations. Waterflooding added at least thirty years of productive life to a majority of these shallow oil wells and increased the percentage of recoverable oil by ten to twenty percent. But the significense is even greater in that dependence

27

upon primary production alone was a thing of the past. In addition to waterflooding, a number of other methods of secondary and tertiary recovery have been successfully put into use since that time. The age of Enhanced Oil Recovery (EOR) had arrived.

While waterflooding from an overall standpoint was successful, it was not an exact science and the results were by no means uniform. This was partly due to the varying formations into which the water was injected. But it was also due to the different methods and pressures employed in implementing this relatively new way of recovering some of the remaining oil in the ground.

Some reservoir engineers apparently took the "more is better" approach, i.e., if one-thousand pounds injection pressure is good, then two-thousand should be twice as good. This concept often proved not only erroneous, but sometimes counter-productive. There is a tendency for very high pressures to channel and by-pass some of the oil that hopefully would be pushed toward the producing wells.

In one instance a major oil company used very high injection pressures. Their own results were something less than rewarding. But a small independent whose lease was about a mile from the point of injection reaped the benefits. He drilled several good producers on some open locations along a line adjoining the major's lease. The major had literally pumped their oil onto the independent's lease!

In one area it was found that shutting down the injection pumps for a few days at a time actually helped the production from the producing wells. It might be hard to conceive how this could happen. But an examination of the hydraulics, so to speak, of injection should make it easier to understand. When pumping

28

water into a standpipe or overhead storage tank, when the pumps are shut down the only pressure remaining is the hydrostatic head from the height of the water column. But in water injection there is a buildup of pressure in the formation because of the entrained gas and/or air. Hence, a substantial pressure remains after the injection pumps are no longer operating.

In the days when daily allowables for most producing wells in Texas were somewhat less than one-hundred percent of what they were capable of producing, the allowables for most wells under waterflood were one-hundred percent. There were instances when one operator would derive some benefits from water injection on a neighboring lease, but in order for the operator to obtain the full allowable from the Railroad Commission, it was necessary that he do some injection of his own. On small leases this was sometimes not much more than a formality.

I have said that there were times when channeling and by-passing of oil took place. Even under the best conditions quite a bit of this happened. Many operators later found good production by drilling in between their old producing wells. This is called infill drilling.

In 1946, good bourbon whiskey was scarce. During that period my friends and I drank quite a bit of Three Feathers, which was a brand of bourbon whiskey made from potatoes. It wasn't exactly rot-gut, but I have tasted better.

A lot of other iems were scarce at that time - we still had not recovered from World War II. You had to get your name on a list to get any brand of popular new car. Many people had their names of lists for Chevy Fleetlines. Many items sold by oil field supply companies were in short supply, too. Among them were thirty-six inch pipe wrenches, three inch standard tees, spinning chain and many items of pipe nipples. You can imagine our joy when a freight truck drove up to our dock with one or another of these items on it!

## Chapter VII

## THE HENDRICKS REEF

A few miles west of Kermit there is a strip a few miles wide known as the Hendricks Reef. Actually, the strip starts in the vicinity of Eunice, New Mexico, passes through Winkler County and down into Ward County. The significence of this strip of land, as it were, is that at a depth of 3,000 feet, more or less, oil production is available, but in order to produce the oil you have to produce a lot of water with it.

From this formation it has been known for wells to produce a total of 30,000 barrels of fluid per day for a recovery of 100 barrels of oil! In earlier years these large volumes of fluid were produced in a number of ways: casing pumps, operated by pumping units with one inch sucker rods; electrically operated downhole Reda pumps; gas lift and later, air lift, the latter being a method employed by Monsanto Company until a few years ago. But regardless of the method of lifting the fluid to the surface, the same basic way of separating the oil from these large volumes of water was used: that being to pump the fluid into a system of skimming ponds with troughs known as weir boxes used to divert the oil, which being lighter than the water, rose to the surface of the ponds, into one area, and the water by gravity entered a system of canals which led to a reservoir just west of the town of Wink and which was known as Wink Falls. The city of Wink was completely surrounded by the canals. When entering Wink from any direction it was necessary to cross one of them. At these crossing points cattle guards were built. The Hendricks Reef has produced millions of barrels of oil, in the past fifty years, and is still producing.

However, in the 60's the Texas Railroad Commission issued an order requiring the oil operators in the area to discontinue the skimming operations in the open pits, and further, to dispose of the produced water in zones in the formation that could not possibly contaminate the fresh water zones nearer the surface.

This order was vigorously opposed by the affected oil operators, but to no avail. The contention of the operators was that if the Hendricks produced water had not contaminated the fresh water zones in the thirty plus years that it had been producing prior to that time, that it never would.

Notwithstanding, the operators, at considerable expense, had to install either lined skimming pits or a system of rather large storage tanks to handle the large volumes of produced fluid previously handled in the open ponds or tanks and also had to drill injection wells to dispose of the produced water. This also entailed injection pumps to force the water into the formations selected for disposal purposes. Needless to say, this was the end of Wink Falls and the systems of canals that fed it. I should add that the produced water contained H2S and was therefore highly corrosive.

In passing we should say that in this area the Hendricks Reef strip is also the boundary between the Permian Basin and the Delaware Basin. I am not a geologist but I do know that in a distance of a mere ten miles or so the Ellenberger section is found at a depth of 11,000 feet approximate in the Permian Basin, whereas it is reached at a depth of 22,000 feet in the Delaware Basin.

31

## Chapter VIII

## MENTONE AND LOVING COUNTY

It would be an injustice, I think, not to at least make mention of Loving County, just west of Winkler County, and its County Seat, Mentone, some thirty-three miles southwest of Kermit. I am sure that my good friends in the area would notice the omission. This county has an area of 648 square miles and a population of 91!

In the forty-two years since I moved to West Texas, I have made many friends in Loving County. I will try to name some of them: the Moorheads; Bob and Ann Capps; the Creagers; the Oscar Williams; The Whatleys, the Hoppers; the Wheats; the Hartleys; the Ash Williams; the Wilkersons; the Keenes (how could anyone forget Newt); the Massingills; the Elgin (Punk) Jones; and the Wilsons. I am sure that I have missed some and for that I beg forgiveness. I know, too, that many of those I have named are no longer among the living. I pray for God's blessings upon all of them.

A number of exciting and interesting events have happened in Mentone and the surrounding area in the intervening years. Like when Albert Whatley poured gasoline on a bush and set fire to it to get rid of some wasps or other bees. When he lit the fire it also caught his clothes afire. Like most people with burning clothes, he ran. But Mrs. Whatley ran after him. She tackled him and managed to extinguish the blaze. As it was, he was pretty badly burned, but he did survive. If she hadn't been there I believe he would have been a goner. Bear in mind, that when Mrs. Whatley made that life-saving tackle, she was at least seventy years old.

The Whatleys pretty well kept up with what their neighbors were doing. Mrs. Whatley had a pair of field glasses. She would stand in her yard and look around and see what all was going on in the neighborhood.

The original shallow production in the Mentone area — known as the Wheat Field — for the most part was drilled in the 1920's. Its approximate average depth was 4,400 feet. When I came to Kermit in 1946 this field had been producing for 20 years. These wells had been drilled with cable tools and in fact, many of them were still being pumped with the old bullwheel units. These operations used wooden derricks, the same ones that were used when drilling the wells. These gradually gave way to conventional walking beam type pumping units as we know them today. In 1966 the late Robert O. (Bob) Moorhead donated one of these wooden derricks to the City of Kermit, who moved it to Pioneer Park in that city, where it still stands. Our thanks to Bill Beckham and the Winkler County News for the accompanying photo of the derrick.

In the Forties I was told that reservoir engineers had concluded that the Delaware Sand, the pay section in the original Wheat Field, according to their calculations should have been depleted by that time, but it was still producing then, and for that matter, still is. It has been suggested by some that this pool was fed by an underground stream of some kind, in somewhat the same manner that, some believe, the Hendricks Reef is fed.

Of course, since the twenties, wells have been drilled in Loving County to pay sections other than the Delaware Sand, including a number of deep gas wells that have been drilled in the last twenty years.

## Chapter IX

## MESQUITE BUSHES AND SOME OTHER THINGS

In West Texas and Southeast New Mexico, the mesquite bush is pretty commonly seen except where it has been exterminated. I have been told that it is not native to this area, but migrated northward from Mexico something over a hundred years ago, this migration taking place by way of the cattle being driven north, sometimes by Apache Indians, who had appropriated the cattle from their Mexican owners. Mesquite wood, both the above ground portion and the roots, is excellent for barbequing. It is also considered to be the best weather prophet available in the Spring. It is said that when the mesquite blooms there will be no more killing freezes in a given spring, so your gardens and fruit trees are safe. I have been told, however, that the mesquites were fooled on two occasions, in the memory of living man. They had come out in full bloom and then there were bad freezes. The mesquite is considered a nuisance because they use so much water to the detriment of other vegetation. They have very long tap roots and enough of them can lower the water table in a given area.

In several counties in West Texas, among them Winkler and Loving Counties, the section lines do not run due north and south and east and west, but diagonally to those points. The streets and most of the houses in Kermit are accordingly laid out. To someone not familiar with this fact, the legal description of a piece of property can be very confusing. It might read something like this: The North Quarter of the East Quarter of the South Quarter of Section 16, etc. I have heard several explanations for this part of the country being laid out in that manner, but I believe the most commonly accepted one is that the Texas

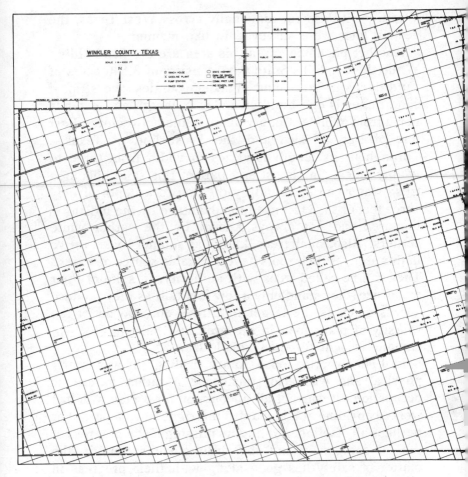

*A Plat of Winkler County. [Note how the section and township lines run diagonally]*

and Pacific Railway Company, which owned much of the land on both sides of the railroad right-of-way, did much of the land surveying in the area, and used their railway as their reference point and since the railway tracks from Ft.

35

Worth to El Paso cut diagonally across West Texas, the section lines were surveyed in like manner.

Another phenomenon in this area are the Sand Hills. While the Sandhills State Park consists of 3,840 acres of sand dunes in Ward and Winkler counties, the strip of sand dunes is one hundred miles in length and extends north from Winkler County along a line between the East line of New Mexico and the West line of Texas. Throughout its length it varies in width from three to twenty miles. In almost any part of this sand hills area fresh water can be found by digging to a depth of only three feet or so, a fact used to advantage by the Indians in the area and not always known by the earlier white settlers. Also, small trees, known as shinnery oaks, thrive in this area, as their roots have a reliable source of water. They can be called trees with authority, in spite of their small size (they stand only a few feet tall) as they produce acorns much as the larger oak trees do. No doubt the sparsity of plant food in the area and perhaps the arid climate account for their small size.

In 1946, working on a rotary drilling rig was pretty physical and was also considered a rather hazardous occupation. It was not all uncommon for a man who had worked any time at all on a drilling rig to have a part(s) or perhaps all of a finger or fingers missing. The progress of the oil companies and the drilling contractors in the matter of safety has gone along with their progress in other areas. Equipment design is safer, many safety devices are standard equipment on most drilling rigs and a greater safety consciousness exists, all of which have broght about a much safer place for the drilling crews to work in.

In considering the number of people involved in the exploration for and production of oil, we have not discussed the chain reaction resulting from their

*A Photo of the Sandhills in Winkler County [Courtesy of Sorrells Photo Shop]*

employment: The barbers, dentists, doctors, grocery clerks, bank clerks and others. The accepted ratio on this, I think, is four to one. That is, for every person gainfully employed in an industry in a town, four more people will eventually find employment.

But the ripple effect doesn't end at the city limits of Kermit, Midland, or Odessa, or for that matter, at the state lines of the major oil producing states. Many jobs in Cleveland, Ohio; Pittsburgh, Pennsylvania; Kansas City, Missouri; Little Rock, Arkansas; Detroit, Michigan; and some other places not otherwise identified with the oil and gas industries are affected because much of what they produce is sold in the oil field.

*A Windmill on the Frying Pan Ranch — In Operation Since 1929*

## Chapter X

## A MISUNDERSTOOD INDUSTRY

Why is the petroleum industry so misunderstood, or more precisely, less understood, by people not associated with it? To a great extent it is our fault, really, in that over the years we have done such a lousy public relations job. We have told ourselves about our importance to the overall economy and to our national security, we have told ourselves about our problems, but we have not carried these messages to the general public. You could read about it in the Oil and Gas Journal or in World Oil, but it wasn't in Newsweek. You could read about it in Midland, Odessa, Ft. Worth or Dallas daily newspapers, but not in the St. Louis, New York City, Washington, D.C. or Boston papers. And we did very little to dispel the fantasy that the oil patch was full of instant millionaires and that oil wells gushing liquid gold were commonplace. Things are now moving in the right direction. Major oil companies, for the past several years, have been carrying full page ads in weekly and monthly popular publications, not just saying that they have better oil and gas than their competitors, but also telling the story of the oil industry itself. This is certainly good, but it is long overdue. We have much more to do in this respect.

I recall being taught about cotton and wool and coal, in school, their origin, how they were produced and processed, but I don't remember being told anything about oil and gas. Somewhere in our elementary or secondary schools something like this should be included:

"The oil and gas industries have had much mystery and romance attached to them. Much of this is because, like in the gold rushes, there has always been the possibility of the big strike, and there are some rags to riches stories to back it up. But for the most part the oil and gas industries, like coal mining, lumbering and manufacturing, are businesses, with much risk and many problems attached to them. A few facts concerning the petroleum industry are here brought out. First, while geology and seismic studies enable a geologist to make a prediction — an educated quess — of the possibility of finding oil or gas in a given area, there is no certainty that they will be found. The status of the well is not known until it is drilled to total depth. In drilling exploratory or "wildcat" wells the number of successes runs on an average of about sixteen percent, or one out of six wells.

Second, the percentage of wells that flow naturally to the surface is very low. Most of them have to be stimulated by such techniques as hydraulic fracturing or acidizing in order to allow the oil to reach the well bore at the bottom of the well. After this is accomplished the oil may or may not flow to the surface. When it does not, which is often the case, the oil has to be artificially lifted to the surface, the most common method being the walking beam pump jack, or pumping unit, which with "sucker rods" attacked to a pump at the fluid level, usually near the bottom of the well, lifts the oil to the surface. Another fact that should be clarified is that crude oil as it reaches the surface is, as the name implies, a raw material and in that state is not ready for commercial use. It is, in its purest form, a combination of a multitude of hydrocarbon compounds, which must be separated or refined before they can be used in the many familiar ways in which petroleum products are used: gasoline and diesel fuel for our cars and trucks; lubricating oils; paints; synthetic rubber; medicines and many others. It is unusual, however, for even crude oil to arrive at the surface of a well in a pure state. Usually it includes gas mixed with it and often physically mixed with water in the form of an emulsion.

This gas and water must be separated from the crude oil before it leaves the lease on which it is produced. In addition to the above, crude oil often includes certain objectionable compounds such as hydrogen sulphide which have to be removed either before or during the refining process."

"Crude oil is flowed or pumped to refineries to be separated into its various components. Refining is accomplished by a combination of pressures, temperatures and distillation processes much as you will find in the science and chemical laboratories in your school. There are also some other more sophisticated methods such as catalytic cracking used to break down crude oil into its components, but in all cases we are talking about chemistry and physics. For those of you who might want to know more about these processes, there are some well written books on the subject."

You will note that some of the points brought out in the foregoing are that by no means do all wells flow naturally and that crude oil is not ready for commercial use when it reaches the surface. You might be surprised at the number of people who think that somehow oil is ready for human use when it comes out of the ground. This isn't really too hard to understand, as coal, for instance, is in many cases ready for use when it is mined. In addition to getting information of this kind into the textbooks and classrooms of our elementary or secondary schools, it wouldn't do any harm to see that every state governor, every U.S. Senator and Representative received it, too, with particular emphasis on those in non-oil producing states.

In 1946 there were still quite a few cable tool rigs running. There were some in the immediate area of Kermit, a few at Mentone, some in the Grandfalls-Royalty area and quite a few of them running near Artesia in Eddy county, New Mexico. While they were limited as to the depth they could go — 4,500 to 5,000 feet, although there were some that went to as much as 8,000 feet — and they were slow, they were cheaper and many operators preferred them, their contention being that the producing zone was not plugged off by mud as might be the case when drilling with a rotary rig. One of the disadvantages of cable tools was the lack of control if a well blew out. My impression of the old "jar heads" — the cable tool driller and his tool dresser — it that they usually chewed tobacco, didn't have much to say and were rarely in a hurry. They usually didn't work on weekends, either.

The significence of telling the story of the oil and gas industry to the misinformed or less informed people of our country lays not just in letting them know the true economics of our segment of the economy. Many of them are more directly affected than they realize. A paint manufacturer and their employees in Kansas City, tire manufacturers in Akron, Ohio, manufacturers of plastic products in West Virginia or Iowa, manufacturers of drugs in New England, all have more than an academic stake in what happens to the petroleum industry. In many cases we provide not only the raw material, but the energy for their operations. And, as stated before, we are often their customers, too!

The evolution of the natural gas industry is a story in itself. We mentioned earlier that the role of natural gas in the mid forties was minor. It was considered somewhat of a nuisance. Part of it was put to some use, however. In 1946 there were a number of carbon black plants in operations in West Texas and New Mexico. One of the principal uscs of the blacks, as they were called, that were produced by these plants, was for synthetic rubber. The big demand for synthetic rubber was initially created in

*The Sid Richardson Gasoline Company Keystone Gasoline Plant in Winkler County, Texas. This picture was made in 1951. The plant was built in 1948 and 1949. The black smoke in the background was from the old Cabot Carbon Company Keystone Carbon Black plant a few miles to the west. Photo courtesy of Sid Richardson Gasoline Co. and Sorrells Photo Shop.*

World War II, when our primary sources of natural rubber were cut off, when the Japanese invaded Southeast Asia. A number of carbon black plants were built. The largest of these plants was built a few miles west of Odessa, Texas, by United Carbon Company for the Defense Procurement Corporation. After World War II the plant was sold to Sid Richardson Carbon and Gasoline Company. The companies producing the carbon blacks had made contracts with the producers of the gas at a very favorable price at a time when natural gas had very little market potential. But when these contracts expired the demand for natural gas was greater and the economics of manufacturing carbon black from natural gas with the existing process was no longer favorable. Besides, the old gas burning plants discharged a lot of pollutants into the air. The gas burning plants were replaced by the cleaner, more cost efficent plants that made the blacks from crude oil. In the meantime, gasoline plants were removing the light ends from the produced gas and the residue gas was being shipped in big inch pipe lines to the factories and the population centers of the North and East. Also, the petrochemical industry had burgeoned, much of it on the Gulf Coast of Texas.

When speaking of gasoline plants I am reminded of a fellow who worked in one of them something like thirty years ago. We shall call him John. He was a good dependable man, but speed was not one of his strong ponts. He had one speed and that was a slow one. Then one day there was a fire in the plant. It was a small one with no personal injuries and little damage to the plant. But any kind of fire in a gasoline plant is considered serious until it is disposed of. After the fire had been put out and things were getting back to normal, one of the other men who worked in the plant asked John: "Say, didn't I see you running when we had the fire?" "No, I wasn't running," was John's reply, "but I passed some fellows who were running."

We should take time out here to discuss what natural gas is. As with crude oil, natural gas that comes from a gas or oil well is not one element or compound. It is a number of them in combination. Nor is all natural gas the same. In most cases natural gas must be processed in some manner before it can be put to a useful purpose. Also, as in the case of crude oil, certain undesirable impurities are often present that have to be removed before the gas can be safely used.

## Chapter XI

## THE TRAINS AND THE WINDMILLS

In 1946 passenger rail service was still available to West Texans. I rode the Texas and Pacific coaches to Arkansas and back many times. There was still passenger service to Kermit, too. It was called the Texas and New Mexico Railway Company and ran from Monahans, Texas to Lovington, New Mexico. It was actually a branch of the Texas and Pacific Railway Company. Many of the old section houses were still in existence, among them the one at Cheyenne, about nine miles north of Kermit, and Teague Switch, between Jal and Eunice, New Mexico. All of them were destined to be phased out, including the depot at Kermit, and in fact passenger service to our part of West Texas was to be eliminated in a few years. This represented the passing of an era — something that gives me an empty, nostalgic feeling. Of course, freight trains still run, not only on the main lines but on the short line through Kermit as well. And to the south and west of us, on the old Southern Pacific tracks, there is an Amtrak system operating.

I can think of nothing more typical of West Texas than the windmill. Found scattered over the many rangelands of the ranches of the area, they serve a very useful purpose in providing a dependable source of power to pump water from wells for the ranchers' cattle and other livestock. They have the advantage of eliminating the need for electricity and do not require the attention needed by gasoline engines that would otherwise be needed to pump the water. And of course the lifting cost is much less, especially since the energy crunch of the 1970's. There aren't many days in West Texas that there isn't enough wind to operate a windmill, something that

45

would not be true in some other areas. As the water is pumped, it is flowed into large earthen reservoirs or stock tanks. This assures water for the livestock even on days when there is not enough wind to operate the windmill. Incidentally, around a stock tank is not a bad place to hunt dove or quail, during season and with the rancher's permission, of course. In some areas windmills have been used to generate electricity, too.

The cost of maintaining windmills are relatively small. Tom Lineberry, a rancher friend of mine, says he has some windmills that have been running since 1929 with no maintenance needed other than changing the oil in them.

*Tom Lineberry [Frying Pan Ranch]*

## Chapter XII

## A MEMORABLE NEW YEARS DAY

As an employee of Republic Supply Company for thirty-three years, twenty of which were spent in Kermit, I would be remiss, I think, if I did not say something about their old store building that was in Kermit when I went there in 1946 and was used until 1961, when it was torn down and replaced by a new one. The old building was approximately 30 by 80 feet in size. It was a wooden frame structure with a corrugated iron roof. This building was originally owned by the old Atlas Supply Company and had been moved to Kermit from Pyote, which was at one time a supply center for the oil field. Republic added

*The Old Republic Supply Company Store in Kermit [Photo taken in late 1950's]*

a lean-to 10 by 15 foot office on the south side of the building, then later added a lean-to bunkhouse back of the office for their single men employees to live in.

Rains are usually rather rare in this area — around twelve inches mean annual rainfall — but when it did rain the roof leaked. Finally, the leaks got so bad that the Company approved the repair of the roof. It was December of 1947. We had notified the local contractor that we wanted him to do the needed repairs and he said he would have it done as soon as he finished some other work. Christmas came and went. Then New Year's Eve. As I recall, I went out with some friends of mine and saw the old year out and the new one in in good form. I paid for this celebration the following day. Sometime around 8:00 New Year's morning I heard a loud banging sound. In my less than alert condition I couldn't figure out what it was. But by degrees I began to realize what was going on. The man had come to repair the roof! It would have been a miserable morning for me at best but the hammering on the roof didn't help a bit. With my head throbbing, every blow of the hammer sounded like a cannon being fired.

# Chapter XIII

## A TODDY FOR THE BODY

Let's face it! There was a lot of drinking going on back in the 1940's. Not all of the toolpushers were heavy drinkers, but some of those that I knew were. These fellows didn't wait until the cocktail hour to do their drinking, either. Some of them regularly drank a fifth of whisky a day or more. Of course, the toolpushers were not the only ones imbibing in those days, nor has drinking been confined to that period of time.

One time a supply salesman handed one of these good drinking hands a half pint of bourbon. The toolpusher took the cap off the bottle, tipped it up, chug-a-lugged and threw the bottle away. "Thanks for the drink! he said, somewhat contemptously.

In another instance several fellows were talking about someone drinking a pint a whiskey a day. One of these heavy drinkers said: "Hell, I spill more than that in a day!"

A good friend of mine who drank quite a bit experienced some heart trouble. His doctor told him that it might be best if he would slow down on this drinking. He said: "Oh, two or three drinks in the evening before dinner won't hurt you." "Doc," my friend replied, "two or three drinks just makes me thirsty!"

## Chapter XIV

## THE LAND OF ENCHANTMENT

In 1948, I was transferred to Artesia, New Mexico. It was somewhat different from Kermit. As stated before, there were quite a few cable tool rigs running in that area and in fact, we stocked drilling jars, cable tool bits, soft rope, forgie handles and some other items that are used on cable tool rigs.

At Carlsbad there were several potash mines in operation and part of our business was with the mining companies. The Santa Fe Railway runs through Artesia and I saw many a trainload of potash go north to Clovis, New Mexico where it connected with the Santa Fe mainline.

During the two years I was in Artesia I learned to love New Mexico and I still like to go to Artesia, as well as Roswell and Carlsbad.

They call New Mexico the Land of Enchantment. As far as I am concerned it is aptly named. But when you enter the state on Highway 18, about ten miles north of Kermit, a stranger might wonder why anyone would call it "Enchanted." At that point nothing but sand, sagebrush and mesquite greets the eye. And when you cross the state line on Highway 285 — the road from Pecos to Carlsbad — the scenery is not much more impressive. And yet, when I enter the state at either of these points I have a feeling of exhilaration, of excitement. It is something that I have never been able to adequately explain.

Of course, there are many scenic spots in new Mexico: the Caverns, White Sands, the Guadalupe and Sacramento Mountains, located in the northern part of the state.

But perhaps the fascination one feels for the state cannot be explained by the mere word "beauty." We must use words like grandeur, majesty, agelessness. It is the sort of fascination that does not immediately overwhelm the senses. It is something, I think, that typifies much of the West.

## Chapter XV

## ROLL AND WHISTLE

Our store in Artesia was right next to the Santa Fe Railway tracks. As in the other stores that I had worked in, I lived in the store building. Rudy Holman, my friend and fellow employee, had worked in his earlier years for a railway company in Louisiana. As you know, I am sure, railroad cars, regardless of ownership, are moved around frequently from one railroad line to another for reasons of logistics and delivery of merchandise. Also, every rail car has a serial number. Many times when the trains ran past our store Rudy would say: "I remember that car. It used to run on a line that went through Rayne, Louisiana." He knew it by its serial number. Then, every once in a while, as a train went through he would say: "Roll and whistle you S.O.B., you can't walk or sing!"

Rudy and his wife, Isabel, coming from Louisiana, were "Cajuns" in the best tradition. They drank cajun coffee, that dark, almost blue stuff. They drank it in small demitasse cups. But a small cup was enough. Also, Rudy smoked Picayune cigarettes, another product of Cajun country. Now, when you smoked a Picayune, you had smoked a cigarette! Sometimes I would go over to their house on a Sunday morning. They would hand me a cup of their coffee and a Picayune cigarette. I can tell you, the combination of the two put me on a high for the rest of the day!

During the time I lived in New Mexico, multiple completions in a single well bore were not permitted by the New Mexico Oil and Gas Conservation Commission. Since there were a number of productive pay zones, there were places where you would see a number of pumping units operating almost side by side. I've seen as many as six of them operating in this manner. One example of this was on a Skelly lease several miles east of Jal. I believe I could have stood in the center of the location and thrown a

*Rudy Holman [right] with Unidentified Friend At Republic Supply Company's Artesia, N.M. Store.*

rock and hit any of the pumping units! They ranged in size like from D-25 to D-320. Later, the State regulations were relaxed and multiple completions were permitted.

The town of Artesia is in the Pecos River valley. The name Artesia derives from the fact that originally there were many artesian water wells in that area. These wells no longer flow water to the surface.

Going west from Artesia to Hope, Mayhill and Cloudcroft you are climbing into the Sacramento Mountains and to the north of Cloudcroft and west of Roswell is Ruidoso. Of course, at Carlsbad, you are near Carlsbad Caverns and the Guadalupe Mountains. This is truly fascinating country. I never tire of going there.

## Chapter XVI

## HOBBS, NEW MEXICO

In 1950, I was transferred to Hobbs, where I would stay for five years. At Hobbs, Republic Supply Company had a big two-story frame building. The building had been moved there earlier from Pyote, Texas. The ground floor served as the store, the upstairs was for employee living quarters. A family occupied most of the upper floor. I had one room.

Our Hobbs store served a large area. Other than the store in Artesia (which was closed in 1952) it was the only store we had in New Mexico. Then in 1953 Republic opened a store in Farmington, New Mexico, to serve the Four Corners area. In connection with the latter, I spend two weeks in Farmington ordering the inital stock of material for the store there.

While at Hobbs I made many trips to Eunice, Oil Center, Monument, Buckeye, Lovington, Tatum, Roswell and Crossroads. At one time we served a drilling rig on a wildcat location near Santa Rosa, New Mexico. The location was 252 miles from our Hobbs store. During that time I made several trips to the rig. Sometimes I made the round trip in the same day. Those were long days! The well turned out to be a dry hole.

## Chapter XVII

## THE LUNCHEON

One Sunday morning in the early 50's when I was at Hobbs, Ed Patton, toolpusher for Westlund Drilling Co., came by our store for a few things he needed on the rig. It was around 10:30 when he came in but it was about 11:30 by the time we had his order filled. I suggested that we go eat lunch. We went to the Drake Cafe, a big place a block or two east of Turner on Broadway.

I guess you could say we each had a "Blue Plate Special,"but a pretty good lunch at that. While we were having our lunch I got to thinking about how much money I had on me, as I wasn't sure that I could cash a check, since I didn't know the people in the Drake too well.

When we had finished our lunch the waitress brought our check. it was for $3.71. I decided that I had better wait to tip the waitress until I knew how much money I had left after paying the check.

At the cash register I took out my billfold. There were three one dollar bills in it. I reached in my right hand pocket and took out all my change. There were two quarters, a dime, two nickels and a penny — exactly seventy-one cents! This happened unseen by Ed Patton. After I had paid the check we started out the door. I said: "Oh, I forgot to tip the waitress." Ed said: "I left one for her." I was sure glad that he had.

## Chapter XVIII

## GETTING STUCK IN THE MUD AT ROSWELL

The following happened at Roswell, New Mexico. Postelle Drilling Co. had a rig running out on the Caprock between Tatum and Roswell. Wendell Postelle was pushing the rig. One day when I was calling on the rig, Wendell and I decided to go to Roswell for lunch.

It had been raining in Roswell and there was a lot of mud back of the cafe where we parked, as Southern Union Gas Company had done some digging there in connection with laying a gas line. When we came out to our car after lunch, sure enough, we were stuck in the mud. But the boys with Southern Union had a winch truck there for just such an occasion and had us out in no time at all.

After they had gotten us unstuck, they told us about something that had happened the day before that wasn't quite so easy to take care of. It was a panel job driven by a salesman for a steel company out of Albuquerque. When they hooked onto him to pull him out, they strained and strained and finally stripped their winch. They had to go get a larger truck to get him out of the mud.

After they had gotten him out of the mud, they asked him what it was in his vehicle that was so heavy. He had eight and one-half tons of steel: rounds, angles, channels, and bars! It doesn't take much steel to weigh up in a hurry.

# Chapter XIX

## THE GRAND OPENING

When I went to Hobbs the two main hotels there were the Harden and the Frey. The Harden was considered the better of the two. One of the manufacturers representatives who called on our store from time to time always stayed at the Frey when he was in Hobbs. There was a very good reason why he didn't stay in the Harden.

Many years earlier, a short time after the Harden Hotel was built, the management of the hotel held a grand opening. At the time that it was built in 1930 it was considered to be a pretty first class place. A three story affair, it had a large lobby with high ceilings, chandeliers for lighting and nice, thick carpets. For anyone who wanted to make an impression on their clients it was the place to stay. It was real nice to be able to say: "I'll be staying at the Harden." Our salesman friend was spending the night there. During the time that I knew him he didn't drink at all, but at the time of the grand opening he was anything but a tee-totaller. Two of his drinking buddies were also spending the night at the Harden. After consuming quite a bit of whiskey the three of them very definitely got into the spirit of the event. One of them had a gun of some kind and proceeded to shoot out the lights on the chandeliers in the lobby of the hotel. The hotel had wall mounted telephones. One of these fellows literally ripped one of these phones out by its roots, as it were. These men were in the process of making a shambles of the place.

The police were called and the men were ejected from the hotel. I think maybe they spent the rest of the night in jail. Of course, they had to pay for the damage they had done. Further, the three of them were barred for life from staying in the hotel!

*The Harden Hotel in Hobbs, N.M.* [*Photo made in 1973. The structure was condemned in the same year*]

The accompanying photo of the hotel was shot in 1973. The building was condemned by the city authorities the same year. I feel sure that if the walls of the venerable old structure could talk they would be very interesting to listen to.

I am indebted to the Hobbs Public Library for making it possible for me to include a photo of the hotel. They loaned me a negative of the picture. This may possibly be the only one in existance since the hotel was razed sometime in the 1970's.

## Chapter XX

## SLEEPING IN THE BRADY HOTEL

It was during one of the Oil Shows at Tulsa, Oklahoma. I believe it was in 1948. Our company, Republic Supply Company, had sent a number of us store managers and field salesmen to Tulsa to attend the show.

Tulsa was a pretty big city, a quarter of a million I guess. But during the International Petroleum Exposition, as the show was called, housing facilities in the city were taxed to the limit. If you hadn't made hotel reservations at least six months in advance you were just out of luck. Some of the residents of Tulsa, who were going to be out of town during the show, graciously allowed some of us out of town people who didn't have reservations to stay in their homes during the show. I was supposed to stay in one of them, but somehow I missed the boat, and here it was around midnight and I had no place to stay.

After wandering around for an hour or so, on foot and on the city buses, I finally arrived at the Brady Hotel, on the north side of Tulsa. It was my last hope.

Now, the Brady was not located in the plushest part of town. The hotel itself could hardly have been placed in a class with the Mayo or the Hotel Tulsa. On a one to ten rating scale I would have to give it something less than a five.

The desk clerk said they were filled up. I said: "Don't you have something? I've wandered all over Tulsa looking for a place to sleep." Finally the clerk said: "I'll tell you what. I'll fix you a pallet on the landing at the head of the stairs on the second floor."

So there is where I spent what was left of the night. I had a heck of a time getting my outer clothes off, as just about the time I would start to take my trousers off, here would come a girl down the the hall and I would get under the covers quickly. Finally I had gotten tucked in, as it were, but every once in a while another girl would come by my pallet, either arriving or leaving and each of them would look at me rather curiously — the hall light was never turned off.

I shouldn't have worried about offending the modesty of these girls, for it hit me later that these were ladies of the evening. It would have taken a lot more than them seeing me in my skivies to offend their sensibilities!

## Chapter XXI

### TO ELECTRIFY A LEASE

He worked for an independent oil company. He had four pumping wells on forty acre spacing on a one hundred sixty acre tract. He and his family lived in a lease house in the center of the tract.

The wells were very good producers. The power for pumping them was provided by four ZC-503 Fairbanks, Morse Gas engines. Good dependable power — twelve to twenty horse-power range — but they did require some repairs once in a while and sometimes were a little hard to start on cold winter mornings.

The way I made this fellow's acquaintance was that he came into our supply store in Hobbs from time to time to buy parts for his pumping engines: Valves, valve seats, push rods, rocker arms and so forth. Then one day he asked me if I would work up a quotation for all the materials needed to electrify the lease he was pumping. This would involve bringing a power line in to the lease from the main power line, electric motors, automatic controls, and safety shutoff switches. Also, there would be signal lights in his kitchen that would come on whenever one of the four wells was shut down. And there would be remote control switches in his kichen, too, that would enable him to shut down or start any of the wells, should the need arise.

If electrical problems arose he would simply call an electrician. There would be no more repairing of the old ZC-503 engines, and no more cranking them on cold mornings. Pretty neat, wasn't it? He could almost operate the lease from his kitchen table.

The idea was for me to prepare a quotation for him. Then he would present it through channels to the owners of the company. I should say that this was all his idea. The company hadn't asked him to do it. I told him that I would work up the quotation for him, but that I thought that he might be making a mistake, that if his proposal was accepted, they might not need him anymore. They would get a contract pumper to see after the wells for fifty or seventy-five dollars per month for each well. But he insisted upon having the quotation.

I don't know how this turned out as I transferred back to Texas about that time. But I suspect that what might have happened was this: The company would accept his proposal in its entirety, except for the control panel in the kitchen. They wouldn't be needing that nor would they be needing him. He would have proposed and quoted himself out of a job!

## Chapter XXII

## BACK TO KERMIT

In 1955 I transferred back to Kermit to manage the store there. I was to be there seventeen years. As before, I lived in the bunkhouse until 1961 when the new store building was built.

For those of you who are not familiar with the oil field supply business, a supply man is apt to get called at all hours of the day or night and on Sundays and Holidays as well. It was not at all unusual for a customer to come by at 2:00 or 3:00 in the morning for material. We didn't have a doorbell or buzzer, so I rigged up one, using a little bell with an electromagnet on it. A push button switch to mount on the outside of the front door, a six volt battery such as is used on electric hand lanterns and some electrical wire were all that were required. The bell was mounted on the wall near the head of my bed.

Oil field supply men are kind of like firemen — when a phone or buzzer sounds, they react almost automatically. When the little bell rang, I would be on my feet and heading for the front door of the store and still be half asleep. Sometimes I would give the customer what he needed and write up a sales slip and he would be on his way. But if I was very sleepy, I might tell the customer that I would write the sales slip in the morning. In such instances I sometimes woke up in the morning asking myself: "Somebody got some material last night, but who was it and what did they get?" But this usually worked — if I didn't remember, the customer most likely would.

L.D. King worked for Pasotex Pipe Line Company. But he had taken a correspondence course on TV repair and moonlighted as a TV repairman.

63

One morning I told him that I had a problem with my TV — the picture was too dark. "Well," he said, "I'll tell you what to do. On the back of the picture tube there is a little button of sorts. If you will take a screwdriver and kind of scoot the button a little, I believe that will solve you problem."

That night I played my TV for a while, then I said I believe I'd try doing what old L.D. had told me to do. Common sense told me to turn off the TV set and also unplug it at the wall. Nothing like playing it safe. Also, I used a screwdriver with a plastic handle. Then I scooted the button on the back of the picture tube. But I must have let my hand slip or something. Anyhow, I got a pretty good shock.

What I didn't know was that picture tubes hold a charge, somewhat like a condenser, for several hours, even after the TV is turned off. It was a good thing that my feet weren't wet or I might not be around to tell about it.

But L.D. was right, it did clear up the dark picture on my TV.

"Jonsey finally got the key to high-score bowling without bothering to learn the fundamentals!"

## Chapter XXIII

## THE AGE OF THE MINI-SKIRT

It was in Wink, sometime back in the fifties. It was also about the time of the advent of the mini-skirt. A man had just emerged from Chamber's Grocery with a large sack of groceries: potatoes, a head of lettuce, some onions, some canned goods. As he stepped out onto the sidewalk and headed towards his car, he saw a comely looking lady in a mini-skirt approaching from the opposite direction. She so absorbed his attention that he was walking backwards, as it were, towards his auto. He then stepped off the curb with the result that he stumbled and his groceries were spilled — potatoes, onions and all running down the street.

"A TYPICAL DAY WITH THE ENGINEERING DEPARTMENT"

This reminded me of an incident that occured in Hobbs, New Mexico a few years earlier. Two gentlemen motorists, one travelling east on Broadway, the other travelling west on the same street, had a minor fender bumper near the intersection of Broadway and Turner, the primary north and south streets in Hobbs.

Both drivers got out of their cars. One of them said: "It was my fault. I was looking at that good looking gal over on the sidewalk." "Well, what do you think I was looking at?" the other man replied. The two shook hands, got in their respective cars and drove away.

## Chapter XXIV

## RUSSIAN ROULETTE

A foreman for an independent oil company came by our store just about every morning. He smoked a pipe and talked slow — the picture of unhurried deliberation. But when he got in his pickup truck it was a different story. He drove fast enough on the highway and on the county roads, but he didn't slow down on the bumpy lease roads.

A Vee belt salesman, who went out to their lease to check out a complaint, came back to our store scared almost out of his wits. The foreman had carried him around the lease, as he related, going sixty miles an hour over bumps, chuck holes and whatever.

Then one afternoon one of our competitors called us: "I think a customer of yours has been in a serious accident." He certainly wasn't exaggerating. It was the foreman I mentioned above.

To go back a little, the oil company's lease was about twelve miles north and west of town on the west end of what we called Cheyenne Draw. To reach the lease you travelled an oil topped county road. But the county road crossed a so-called butane route — used by the tank trucks hauling flammable materials — about six miles from Kermit. At the point of crossing the butane route the county road had stop signs — the butane route had the right-of-way.

It was at this crossing that the foreman met his Waterloo. A tank truck was heading west on the butane route. At the same instant, the foreman was heading south on the county road. He simply drove under the tank truck. I don't think he suffered any — he probably was killed instantly.

The people who worked and lived in the vicinity of the intersection said that they had seen the man drive to and from the lease every day. They said that he never stopped nor did he even slow down at the stop signs. He cruised through the intersection as though the stop signs did not exist.

I don't know what his philosophy of life and death was, but it seemed to me that he was playing Russian roulette every day, and that on that fateful afternoon there was a bullet in the chamber with his name on it.

## Chapter XXV

## A CROWDED STORE

The old store building was pretty crowded. Our business was improving and our stock of material was being increased. So I started putting some stock in my bedroom: water cans, boxes of wiping rags and the like. Since the bunkroom had been added on the building just behind the office, there was a window between the bunkhouse and the office. When I went from the bunkhouse to the office, I simply crawled through the window. As the office became more and more crowded, I finally moved my desk in the office into the bunkroom. So for a while in the last few years in the old building, prior to the erection of a nice new store building, the bunkroom served as my living quarters, as a store room for stock and as my office!

The lady who worked in the front office at that point in time would prepare reports and documents that required my signature. She would bring them back to my office and lay them on my desk for that purpose. Many times I would see her start to crawl through the window and then decide perhaps that it wouldn't be very ladylike and would go around through the store, which was quite a bit further. Ladies still wore dresses for the most part at that point in time — slack suits and blue jeans hadn't come into their own yet.

In 1961 a new store building was built. It was something we had been needing for a long time. After we had gotten moved into the new building, which was at least twice as large as the old one, I wondered how we had made out as long as we had in the old building. But you simply make do with what you have until you get something better.

## Chapter XXVI

## THE MARK OF A PRO

Back in the sixties I took a week of my vacation time and went with Brother Holt on a trip to northern New Mexico. For him it was a combination business and pleasure trip. He would make his sales calls and between these calls he and I would visit. He had clients in Albuquerque, Grants and Farmington. Of course, at night we visited and had a few drinks. And, on a few occasion, at Navajo Lake in northwestern New Mexico, and at some other places, we did a little fishing.

At Navajo Lake, in particular, I noticed that Holt seemed pretty tired, especially when he was wading out in the water. When we were making sales calls, some of them with people he had never met before, he sparkled as though there was nothing to worry about. But when we got back to the motel where we were staying for the night he looked as though he was about to drop.

It was then, I think, that I first started to appreciate the fact that in selling, as in the theatre, and in the other performing arts, "the show must go on". This concept of professionalism was exemplified as was as anyone could, I think, by Emmett Kelly, the famous clown, who reportedly, just prior to a performance, had gotten word of the death of his mother, and yet went right on with his act.

It is this ability to do his thing, even when he is perhaps not up to it emotionally or physically, that separates the pro from the amateur. I guess you could say that the adrenaline flows when the occasion demands it.

In my case it was years later that I personally experienced this feeling. I began to notice that on a day that I did not expect to be very productive, in fact I had greeted the day with something less than enthusiasm and with almost reluctance, after I got into it I was surprised to find that I had a very good day. I should say here that I learned much earlier not to measure my day in terms of how much I had sold, but by how good my calls had been.

I have had friends at the end of the week ask me: "Did you sell a lot this week?" And I would answer: "I really don't know, but I did have a good week." I said this because I knew that I had made a lot of effective and satisfying calls. If you consistently do that, the sales will come in, other things being equal.

This thing of rising to the occasion and doing your thing, even when you may not feel up to it, is the result of much preparation, practice and mental conditioning over a period of time.

I would like to emphasize, however, that putting on your performance, so to speak, is not one of presenting a canned speech or spiel. It is simply the instinctive performance that an expert or professional in any field will do when the time to do it arrives.

## Chapter XXVII

## THE STUCK PUMP

We repaired a lot of sub-surface pumps at our Kermit store. Sometimes repairing a pump could become pretty physical, especially when the plunger was stuck in the pump barrel or sometimes when the pump was stuck in a joint of tubing. Some of the time we could drive the stuck item out with a bar and a sledge hammer, but if it was stuck too tight we would try to pump it out. We had a Baker two phase hydraulic hand pump that with enough effort we could apply between 5,000 and 6,000 pounds of pressure and often unstick the pump. But sometimes even that wasn't enough.

We had a friend who worked for a company that tested tubing. When we had a particularly tough stuck job, we would call him and he would come by and pump out the stuck item with his high pressure hydraulic pump. In return we would give him old wornout pump barrels from time to time.

One afternoon we had a pump stuck in a joint of 2 3/8" EUE N80 tubing. We washed and we pumped with our Baker pump, but without success. We called our friend with the high pressure pump. He revved his pump up, but nothing happened. He revved it up still higher, but still no unstuck pump. He then went to a still higher pressure and the pump came out of the joint of tubing like a rocket. There was a sound like a screaming Banshee and the pump sailed forty or fifty feet down the alley behind the pump shop. Had there been anyone walking down the alley at that point in time and been in the path of this missile, it would most certainly have beheaded or disemboweled that unfortunate person.

I asked our friend how much pressure he had on his pump. It was something over 13,000 pounds! I said that we would never do that again. If we couldn't get the job done with say 6,000 pounds we would cut it out with a torch or a hacksaw.

Afterward, I told Wayne Hill, production foreman for Texaco (it was their pump) that at least we could say that they had a good joint of tubing, as it stood the test without any damage.

## Chapter XXVIII

## THE NIPPLE CHASERS

We kept a pretty good stock of material in our Kermit store. We tried to have on hand just about everything our customers needed on a regular basis. There were limits to this, of course, and no matter how hard we might try, there were always some things that our customers needed that we didn't have. When that happened we made every effort to get these items for them as expeditiously as possible.

Our immediate and major source of supply was in Odessa, forty-six miles distant. In Odessa there were not only a number of so-called general oil field supply stores, like our own, but quite a few specialty companies: electrical equipment, pumping units and parts, controls and gauges of various kinds, various kinds of tools, and so on. If it was available in Odessa and the customer needed it tomorrow we tried to have it for him by the following morning.

Once the material had been located in Odessa, there was the matter of getting it to Kermit. If it wasn't too heavy or bulky and it was early enough in the day, we would get it put on the bus, which went through Kermit once a day late in the afternoon. But sometimes there was just too much stuff and too many transactions involved and if we were to have it by the following morning someone would have to go after it. A good many times I was the one who made the trip, as I didn't have a family and I would go over to Odessa after hours and maybe have an Italian food dinner or sometimes Chinese food as neither of them were available in Kermit.

Sometimes the boys at Republic's Odessa store would round up the material for us and have it at their store. But quite a few times they didn't have time to do it for us, and I, or whoever else was making the trip, would have to go all over Odessa for it. Bear in mind, there might be as many as a dozen transactions or pickups involved. When it was after closing hours that we went over there, we would work out arrangements such as the following: One company would put the material in a barbeque grill behind their store near the alley, another in their trash can, one put the stuff behind a hedge, one in the mailbox, one company had a metal box behind their warehouse(but outside their fence) especially designed for the purpose. One company would leave the order at an all night service station and another with the cashier at an all night cafe.

In retrospect I have often wondered why, on one of my many trips to Odessa at night, the police didn't stop me and ask me what I was doing when I was driving up and down the alleys, poking in people's trash cans, barbeque grills, mail boxes and so on. I have also thought that I wouldn't dare to do those things now, as the streets of Odessa, Texas are not as safe at 11:00 or 12:00 o'clock at night today as they were at that point in time.

One night I went to Odessa and picked up two lengths of six inch fiberglass pipe. I hauled them on the pump racks on the right hand side of my company car. Weight was no problem, as fiberglass pipe is very light, but length was. This pipe runs around thirty-one or thirty-two feet in length. The legal limit on length, even when properly flagged, was four feet to the rear and three feet to the front of the vehicle carrying the material. As best I can recall, the car I was driving was about twenty-two feet long. I avoided heavy traffic in town. I drove west down Third instead of Second Street, maneuvered past West County Road when there weren't too many cars coming, and so on until I got out of town. Even so, as I was gong west on Third Street, I saw a police car, and the policemen in it saw me too! But they didn't stop me. I have said since that I think that the reason they didn't stop me was that they went into shock. They just couldn't believe their eyes!

Sometimes we needed to make an early morning run to Odessa. If I made the trip I would get on the telephone — we had a direct line to Odessa and Midland — and call the Antler's Motel restaurant. At that time it was run by Mr. Frank Green and was a first-class place to eat. I would tell the cashier that I would be at their restaurant in forty-six minutes — we could legally drive seventy miles an hour in those days — and that I wanted two eggs over medium with ham. When I arrived there and sat down in a booth, the waitress would immediately come out of the kitchen with my order and a cup of coffee. And my breakfast was fresh and hot off the grill!

Sometimes it was necessary to call some of our competitors or other sources of supply in Odessa at night and they would meet me at their place of business. One of them was Misco-United Supply co. One morning about 9:00 A.M. I was in Odessa and went by their store. One of their employees, Pete Kinney, who had met me at their store at night several times, asked me: "Say, doesn't the

74

sunlight hurt your eyes? I thought you only worked at night!''

One Friday night I went to Odessa for a tubing head for Amoco Production Corp. They needed it the first thing Saturday morning.

I didn't leave for Odessa until rather late. By the time I had picked up the tubing head, had dinner at an Italian food restaurant and gotten back to Kermit, it was after midnight.

I decided to deliver the tubing head to the Amoco well that night so I wouldn't have to get up so early the next morning.

The location of the well was about six miles south of Kermit, on a lease road about a mile south of the Wink cutoff from the Monahans highway.

I was driving down the lease road when I saw in my rear vision mirror that a vehicle with two spotlights was bearing down on me pretty fast. I pulled off to the side of the road and waited. It was Cecil Odom, with West Texas Gathering Company. There had been a lot of stealing of mercury from their mercury gas recorders along about that time. He didn't know who was in the car and thought it might be one of the thieves.

## Chapter XXIX

## PECK WILLIAMS AND DOCTOR DUNN

OCS — Oil Country Specialties — manufactured oil well pumping units, as the saying goes, way back when. They designated the sizes of their units by the names of waterfowls. There was a Drake, a Gander, a Duck, a Goose and I think, maybe some others.

Peck Williams was Republic Supply company's representative for the Lubbock, Texas area. One of his customers was Dr. Sam G. Dunn, who, in addition to being a physician of high repute in the area, had considerable oil production in the vicinity of the town of Post, in Garza County and also in the Kermit area. Dr. Dunn and Peck were very good friends and he leaned on Peck quite a bit for advice, especially when buying used material.

One night Dr. Dunn called Peck. "Peck, would give a thousand dollars for a second-hand Goose?" "Well, I might," Peck replied, "but it would have to be the Goose that laid the golden egg!"

One afternoon at our Kermit store I took a telephone call from Dr. Dunn. The purpose of the call was to ask us to deliver a message to one of his pumpers, who lived in a camp, about eight miles northwest of Kermit. I said we would be glad to deliver it, but after hanging the phone up I discovered that all of our company vehicles were gone. But Marvin Parker, the salesman in our area for W.C. Norris Manufacturer, happened to be at our store on one of his visits and said he would run me out there.

When we arrived at the camp, which consisted of three houses, there was no one at the house where the pumper lived. His wife was visiting a neighbor two doors down. There was a little dog in the yard. He did a lot of barking, but looked innocent enough to me. I might also say that I usually get along pretty well with dogs. The man's wife had seen us and came running toward her house. I soon found out why she was running. I had gotten out of the car and left the door on the passenger side of the car open. I said to the lady: "I didn't figure your dog would bite." She said: "Oh, yes, he will!" That seemed to be the little dog's cue to do his thing. You know: "You heard the lady, she just said I was a bad dog!" He snarled and showed his teeth — I swear I didn't know a little dog could have so many teeth — and headed my way. In the meantime I was walking rather briskly — I wouldn't dare run, if I had he would have nailed me for sure — toward Marvin Parker's car, but he had closed the door of his car. The lady had meanwhile called her dog, which is probably all that save me from getting bit.

As we drove back to town I asked Marvin why he had closed the door to his car. "I didn't want that little S.O.B. in the car with me," was his reply.

## Chapter XXX

## LARCENY IN THE OIL FIELD

I have said that there was no basic evil in the oil field, such as existed in organized crime. There was however, some larceny there.

One report that I heard — I am sure there were other instances — concerned an independent operator whose lease adjoined one belonging to a major oil company.

The independent laid a buried flow line and teed into a large diameter buried flow line belonging to the major. He had a lubricated plug valve on his line so that he could be selective in the times that he partook of his neighbor's oil. This significantly enhanced the production from his lease. I would suggest that he might have had the cooperation or help from some of the major's employees in making the tie-in. And I would venture to say that this sort of thing happened at other places as well.

Another form of larceny — stealing, if you will — concerned an operator who not only had some production in which he was the sole owner, but also had leases in which he had partners. When he needed to pull the pump on one of his own wells, quite often he would charge the pulling unit bill and pump repair to one of the partnership wells. This worked especially well when the partners lived in some distant city. Again, I don't think that this was necessarily an isolated case.

There are quite a few ways of stealing other than robbing a bank. Take for instance the following example. Of course, I won't use any names. Also, I will say that I didn't personally witness this, but was told about it by what I would consider a reliable source.

This fellow would go to the lumber yard on Saturday afternoons when they were closed for the weekends. The yard was not fenced in so there was no problem as to access into the yard.

He had a cardboard sign which read: "I am in the yard getting some boards," followed by his name. He attached this to a building near the point of entrance with some thumb tacks. When he had loaded the boards onto his pickup, he drove out to where he had placed his sign. He looked both ways, up and down the street, and then removed the sign from the building. And drove away. Transaction completed!

I was told that this happened, not just once, but a number of times.

## Chapter XXXI

## ANOTHER FORM OF LARCENY, THE NEW DESIGN SUB-SURFACE PUMP

We shall call the man Mr. Smith, although that wasn't his real name.

He worked for an independent oil company. His was an office job, handling the various reports needed for the area in which he worked: production of the oil and/or gas from the wells and other data needed not only by the home office of the company but also by the Texas Railroad Commission. In short, he was the clerk in their local area office.

But he was a pretty sharp cookie and his knowledge extended beyond the papers that he was shuffling. He had a fair idea of what was happening in a pumping or flowing oil well and had an understanding of the problems of lifting oil from the producing formation to the surface.

It was thus that he conceived the idea of a design for a sub-surface pump — a design utterly different from anything any pump manufacturer had even dreamed of.

This was no mere fantasizing on the part of Mr. Smith. He drew specifications and drawings of the pump, including an explanation of the principle of the design, its modus operandi, so to speak.

Since he lacked the financial resources to manufacture and market his invention he approached a sub-surface pump manufacturer, with the proposal that they do these things for him and that he would participate in the venture in the form of a royalty.

The local representative of the pump company sent his drawings and spec sheets to their home office for their consideration. In a few weeks he returned these exhibits to Mr. Smith. "Mr. Smith," the representative said, "my people have looked over your design. They think you have a pretty good idea, but they don't see where there is a present application for it."

Of course, they had shot copies of his papers and drawings and had secretly begun some followup research on his idea. They would wait a few years, make a few changes in the design, just in case he had applied for a patent, and then put it on the market.

They had, in fact, stolen his invention.

# Chapter XXXII

## THE STORE MANAGER'S SCHOOL

In 1958 our company conducted a number of two week training seminars or classes for branch store managers. The purpose of this school was to improve our knowledge and insight into management, and at the same time to increase our awareness of the various departments in the home office. For the latter reason and perhaps some others, the classes were held in Oklahoma City, where our home offices were located.

There were three of us from our district: Jack Miller from Hobbs, Bobby Newton from Big Spring and myself from Kermit. Of course there were others there from some of the other districts.

I thought that these seminars were a good thing. I know that they did me a lot of good.

One event does, however, stand out more importantly in my mind than any other during our stay in Oklahoma City. George Steinmeyer was our mentor, or overall coordinator of the program. Toward the end of the first week he told us men from the field stores that we would be having a luncheon in the company dining room on the following Tuesday. He suggested that we wear a suit and tie for the occasion as we would be joined at the luncheon by a number of company executives.

On Tuesday morning we had our usual sessions on one or the other of the various management techniques. Then, just before 12:00 we went to the dining room. Now, we didn't just sit down anywhere. We were seated according to a predetermined arrangement: a man from the field, then next to him an executive, then another man from the field, then another executive, and so on around

*Mr. W. J. McWilliams, President, Republic Supply Company*

the table. It was my first and only exposure to a "working luncheon".

I would start to take a bite of food and the vice-president next to me would ask me a loaded question about conditions at the Kermit store or what I thought about this or that. I would answer his question and would be ready for another bite and here came another question. This was going on all around the table, at which perhaps a dozen people were seated. After four or five questions, the executive next to me stopped asking questions and so did the others, except the President of the Company, Mr. McWilliams. He was asking questions, too, but he seemed to be moving around the table from one of the boys from the field to the next. It looked like there would be three or four of them before he got to me. But he fooled me! I had just gotten a bite of roast beef when he skipped those other fellows and hit me with a question. I chewed and chewed and chewed and finally answered his question.

Later, one of the department heads in the home office

told me that this was a typical noonday luncheon. As he put it, it was just a way of getting another hour's work out of them. He said he and the other department supervisors didn't have to eat there, but did have to pay for the meal. He called it ulcer alley.

After I had gotten back to West Texas, I told Jelly Ellis, our District Manager, that I was willing to work long hours, day or night, Sundays or Holidays, but that I didn't want any S.O.B. bothering me while I was trying to eat.

Several months later Mr. McWilliams was in West Texas on a visit. He and Jelly Ellis came by the Kermit store. Mr. McWilliams said to me: "Lee, I hear you're mad at me." "No, not really," I replied. I knew then that Jelly had told him what I had said about working luncheons.

But I think what I had said did have an impact. Not long afterward, the dining room in the Oklahoma City office was closed. Also, whenever Mr. McWilliams came to West Texas to one of our sales meetings, he would allow no discussion of business during a luncheon or dinner. And after we had finished eating we would move to another room for our sales meeting sessions.

# Chapter XXXIII

## A MATTER OF OPINION

It was some time back in the 1960's. I had been called for jury duty. It was a condemnation case, to establish a fair value for damages done to a rancher's property by an electric power company crossing the land with their power line to provide electricity for an oil lease. It was not a matter of trespassing as the oil lease agreement gave the operator the right of eminent domain.

The case was an interesting experience in perspective, in differing opinions.

From the rancher's point of view, it was very valuable property, indeed, with industrial possibilities. The expert witness for the rancher said the land was worth two hundred dollars per acre.

The expert witness for the power company took a quite different view of the property. To him it was typical semi-desert land with very little on it but mesquite, sage brush and sand. He placed a value of seven dollars per acre on the property.

At the time of the hearing I could not believe that two intelligent people could differ so greatly in their opinions. I actually thought that these people were sincere in their evaluations.

I realized later that it was simply a matter of horse trading. Both parties to the suit expected to settle for something in between the two figures.

As best as I can remember, we arrived at a figure of sixty-five dollars per acre.

## Chapter XXXIV

## A TEXAN GOES TO OHIO

In December of 1972 I was transferred to New Concord, Ohio to manage the store there. The main purpose of my going up there was to train younger personnel. My track record in that respect had been pretty good, I guess. When I arrived in Ohio there was no one working in the store who had more than three months experience. My work was cut out for me! I should say that Mr. Lee Stallard, an experienced, top-notch salesman was there to help in running the operation. Without him it would have been a formidable task, indeed.

I was supposed to be in Ohio for around eighteen months, or at the most two years. I actually stayed for a little over six years.

My moving to Ohio was the best thing that could have happened to me. I had been running a pretty successful operation in Kermit for seventeen years. Maybe it was too smooth an operation — there wasn't enough challenge. I had gotten in a rut!

There was certainly enough challenge in Ohio. Besides the personnel problems to be coped with, Ohio was a completely different world. The drilling programs consisted primarily of shallow gas wells, ranging in depth from 4,000 to 5,800 feet, depending upon the surface elevation. Where in West Texas the gas wells for the most part were deep — 15,000 to 22,000 feet or more, and a well that produced less than two million cubic feet of gas a day was hardly thought of as a commercial well, while in Ohio a million cubic well was considered to be a very good one, indeed. In fact, a quarter of a million cubic feet was considered quite good and there were thousands of wells producing less than that!

*Republic's New Concord, Ohio Store*

Of course it didn't cost nearly as much to drill a Clinton well in Ohio, since they weren't nearly as deep, costing no more than a tenth on the average as a deep well in West Texas. And another thing — almost one-hundred per cent of the gas and oil in Ohio is sweet. No hydrogen sulphide! You could pull casing that had been in a well for six years and still read the mill marks! Well pressures were quite a bit less too, so well head equipment, valves and fittings were less expensive. In 1972 a typical Clinton well could be drilled, completed and equipped for less than $200,000.

The logistics in Ohio were quite different from West Texas, too. These differences were dictated by the terrain, the climate and economics. Most of eastern Ohio, where I was located, is pretty hilly. The average annual rainfall is 38 inches. The soil is not sandy like in West Texas, but a form of clay that becomes very sticky when it rains. The budget of a well that might, at the most, produce only a quarter of a million cubic feet of gas per day, just wouldn't allow building a large pad of limestone (they don't have caliche in Ohio) to put the rig and the pipe racks on, or building roads to the location. So on almost all locations a bulldozer, sometimes two, was used to move the rig in and out of the locations and to pull the pipe trucks in. Because of this situation, when the customer ordered the casing for the well we always had to be sure which way the couplings on the pipe should be loaded on the trucks that hauled the pipe.

And directions to locations were very important. In an area where you have lots of hills and trees, you can be within a few hundred yards of a small drilling rig (and most of the rigs in Ohio were small) and not be able to see it. To further complicate matters, Ohio is very heavily populated, with many small farms and with many state, county and township roads. Maps are a must up there! And when I say maps, I am not talking about maps of the state or even of the counties, but of township maps! We had dozens of these maps. After all, we were the only Republic store east of Illinois, so we had to serve all of Ohio and sometimes more. You can imagine my confusion when I first moved up there. I had been living in a country where there very few trees, where the terrain was level and where you could see for thirty miles or more on a clear day. But I studied the maps a lot and on weekends did a good deal of scouting out roads and locations and I got pretty good at knowing and giving directions to locations. One native Buckeye told me that I had gotten to know the country better than he did!

Quite frankly, I liked Ohio. Of course I knew that I would be moving back to Texas, God willing, but during my tenure up there I can honestly say that I enjoyed it. And I made a lot of good friends!

When I left Kermit in 1972 the oil field in West Texas was anything but booming. Business was pretty good in Ohio, but this was due more to certain peculiar circumstances, including one large captive account, than to the overall situation. Another thing that favored our business in Ohio was that a number of steel companies and manufacturers, among them Republic Steel (our parent company), U.S. Steel, Ford Motor Company and General Motors, had embarked upon self-help programs to provide assured gas supplies for their own operations. And when the Arab oil embargo and the energy crunch hit in 1973, these programs became even more important.

## Chapter XXXV

## A LAND OF PROMOTERS

Ohio was a land of independent oil operators and promoters. Major oil companies accounted for a very small percentage of the business at our New Concord store. This situation created opportunities and at the same time problems. Generally speaking you can retain more of your profit when dealing with independents. But credit can become a problem. There are many solid, creditworthy independent oil and gas operators, but mixed in with them are some that are not. In fact, some of them are nothing less than shysters. During the six years I was in Ohio I received a liberal education in credit matters. There were some who would pay, but you had to "jack them up" from time to time to get your money. It took a little work but these were still desirable accounts. But then there were some whom you had best get your money from before you delivered the material. And there were some with whom you would insist upon a Bank or

Cashier's check or the long green stuff! It is probably best to avoid accounts in these last categories, but we did quite a bit of business with some of them anyway.

At that time investment in oil and gas ventures were pretty good tax shelters. If an oil venture proved successful, that was fine. But if it didn't you still had a tax shelter. A promoter would put together a "package" consisting of a number of gas wells to be drilled. He would then go out and sell interests in this package to people of means: wealthy doctors, lawyers and businessmen. The way the deal was set up the promoter would collect a fee of X number of dollars for every well in the package that was drilled, this regardless of how good the well was. I guess you might call this a promotional fee, a commission or a finder's fee. If he had a 30 well package and his fee was $5,000 per well, he would derive $150,000 in fees from the package. Not bad work if you can get it, is it? Of course, the cost of drilling the well was paid for by the investor's money.

One of the things that at least one promoter did to impress prospective investors was to enact a little drama on Sunday mornings that he privately referred to as Sunrise Services. He would invite several of them to come down from Pittsburgh or Cleveland or wherever to see what a gas well was like. This would usually be on a Sunday morning. Several days prior to their expected visit he would pick out one of his better gas wells, shut it in and let the gas pressure build up.

Then early that morning he would take his guests out to the well. First, he would point to the pressure on the guage on the well head, which was pretty impressive in itself. Then he would open a wing valve on the well head a little. The gas would whistle through the valve. To the visitors, most of whom had never been near a gas well, it was an unforgetable event. And a good many of them

89

could hardly wait to get a piece of the action in the package that the promoter had put together.

## Chapter XXXVI

## THE CAPTAIN ON THE BRIDGE

Charles Briden was Field Superintendent for Stocker & Sitler, Inc., an independent oil and gas operator with headquarters in Newark, Ohio. Their field operations were conducted by Mr. Briden from a little place near New Philadelphia, Ohio.

I say conduct. Conduct he did, like the conductor of a symphony orchestra, but his mien, I think, was more like that of the captain of a ship.

He ran a smooth operation. One of the reasons for this was that he planned everything. And he carried a blueprint of these plans around in his head. He also had a good sense of logistics and of timing — knowing just when certain things needed to be done. These qualities are especially important in Eastern Ohio for, as discussed earlier, the logistics of drilling wells there are quite a bit different from those in West Texas. So he needed certain items of pipe on location at a certain time, no later, but not much earlier either. And so on for the frac tanks, the oil storage tanks, the separators, and the rest of the equipment needed to equip the well.

Mr. Briden arose from bed at 3:00 A.M. and, with a pot of coffee in front of him, proceeded to plan his day. When his secretary arrived at the office around 7:30, he was ready to start the show. He would stand there in the office with his arms folded and would turn to her and say: ''Call such and such supply company and have them deliver fifteen hundred feet of 8 5/8 to such and such well. Call the tank company and have them deliver two 210's and one horizontal separator to such and such well. Call such and such supply company and have them deliver forty-eight hundred feet of 1 1/2 inch tubing to such and such well.'' And so on. He might have a half dozen or more wells in various stages of drilling and completion. But he was on top of what was going on at all of them.

## Chapter XXXVII

## A DIFFERENT TERRAIN

Because of the hilly terrain, the type of soil and the heavy precipitation in southeastern Ohio, "cats" and four-wheel drive vehicles were a necessity. Some locations were otherwise completely inaccessable.

I had occasion to go to one well just east of Cambridge. It was at the top of a steep hill and on the way up there it was very muddy. A cat driver said he would take me up there. As we went up the hill I looked back down. It seemed almost straight down. When I got through with my business up there I wanted to walk back down, but it was so muddy that I went on the cat. But I was sure glad to get off that hill.

I went to another location with a friend of mine who had a four-wheel drive pickup. The location was in a pit of sorts. We rocked and rolled around getting to the location. There were times when I thought we were going to turn over. I swore that I would never do that again.

A lot of people have a misconception of cats and four-wheel drive vehicles and their limitations. Sure, they can get in and out of places where other vehicles cannot, but they can be turned over. An insurance man in New Concord had a small farm a short distance from town. One Saturday afternoon he was out there on his farm on his farm tractor doing some work on a hillside field. The tractor turned over on top of him and killed him. I heard of another similar accident while I was in Ohio.

A pumper friend of mine saw after some hard to reach wells. In the summer months and other open weather times in the year he carried his motorcycle in the back of his pickup to use in getting to these wells. In the winter when there was snow on the ground he carried a snowmobile for the same purpose.

## Chapter XXXVIII

## THE BIG INTERCHANGE

At Cambridge, Ohio, where Interstates 77 and 70 cross each other, there is the largest highway interchange in the world. It covers something like two sections of land. I-77 goes north from the interchange to New Philadelphia, Dover, Canton and Cleveland. From the interchange it goes south through West Virginia, Virginia and into the Carolinas. I-70 goes east to Washington, D.C. Travelling west it continues through Ohio, Indiana, Illinois, St. Louis and on west to the far western states.

In the course of taking care of company business it was necessary for me to make quite a few trips to Cleveland, Canton and New Philadelphia. Usually I would go east on I-70 to the interchange and take I-77 north. When I would get back to New Concord from one of these trips I would tell the people in the store that it didn't take me as long to come back as going up there. They would then look at kind of funny, like maybe I had slipped a cog or something. But it was true. Going up I would be taking the outer, longer way on the interchange, coming back I would be on the inner side of the interchange. It was two miles closer!

## Chapter XXXIX

## THE PIPE CRUNCH

In 1974 the pipe crunch hit!  And it hit almost overnight.  The casing used for the oil string on most of the gas wells in Ohio was 4 1/2" OD 9.50 lb ST&C K55 Seamless or J55 Electric Weld in Range 2.  The going price was $1.36 per foot delivered to the location.  And before the crunch hit we were begging our customers to buy it!  Then, in a matter of weeks we had all of our casing committed and were trying to get more.

During that period of time we had telephone calls from companies who hadn't previously chosen to give us any business, but who now wanted to buy casing from us.  And we had calls from people we had never heard of before!

Had I chosen to do so, I could have feathered my nest during that time.  I had several people approach me in this manner:  "If you'll get me a string of casing, there will be something in it for you.  And I don't mean Republic, I mean you!"  You understand, of course, that they were prepared to pay for the casing, so there was no idea of misappropriating it, but it would have represented a conflict of interest on my part.  When approached in this manner, I would tell them:  "Well, Republic pays my salary.  I'll try to get you a string, but I don't want anything in return except your good will and future business for Repubic."  But from what I have heard, there was probably a lot more hanky-panky going on than one would dream of, and by some people whom you wouldn't suspect.

One thing for sure, there was a lot of black market casing and tubing sold.  The going price for 4 1/2" casing for Republic and the other pipe manufacturers went up a

93

little to something like $1.60 per foot. But the same size and grade of pipe sold on the black market for as high as $7.00 a foot. A good many of the Clinton gas wells were pretty well depleted after being produced six years. As stated earlier, this casing was, for all practical purposes still new. So a number of operators would pull the casing from these wells and sell it on the black market. Then, for their own drilling program they would buy what casing they could from a legitimate supply company like Republic for $1.60 a foot. In effect, they were buying this casing from a supply company at the going price and selling it in the black market for anywhere from $5.00 to $7.00 per foot!

There just wasn't any way we could meet the needs of our traditional customers for casing and tubing, much less the Johnny come latelys! The steel mills couldn't keep up. After all, 4 1/2" OD 9.5 lb K55 or J55 casing was just one of many sizes, weights and grades of casing that were in big demand, not just in Ohio but in other areas of the oil field as well. To bridge this gap, at least partially, we had a machine shop in Salem, Illinois thread plain end electric weld line pipe in sizes 4 1/2" and 8 5/8" with 8 Round thread and buck on couplings for us. Of course, this casing was tested too, to something like fifteen hundred pounds, as best as I can remember. We then had this trucked into Ohio. This was a lifesaver. We later found a shop in Ohio to do this for us, which was a lot better, logistically, then the one in Illinois, which was approximately 500 miles from New Concord. These operations enabled us to provide casing for a lot of Ohio Clinton gas wells and keep quite a few of our customers happy, too. Of course there were a few of them who leaned on us pretty heavy during the crunch, then forgot about us later when prime pipe was easy to get. But I think most of them appreciated what we had done, and particularly since we had't held them up price-wise.

My pet peeve was — and still is — those companies who bought foreign casing, sometimes at a very small savings. In the case of the 4 1/2'' casing, we lost sales to foreign competition for a difference of less than ten cents a foot. On an average Clinton well that would represent a savings of less than $500. And it was just that much contributing to our national trade deficit. And those same people were enjoying all the fruits and benefits of living and doing business in the greatest and the freest country the world has ever known!

I recall one instance when I was soliciting an account for some of their oil well casing business. The customer put me off by saying that he felt that he owed it to a certain foreign competitor to buy from them since they had earlier provided his company with some casing when they needed it.

I found it difficult to share this fealty, this allegiance, as our company, a scant three years earlier, had rescued this same company from their tubular goods problems by providing them with some of the aforementioned electric weld casing that we had gone to considerable pains to furnish. Also, I could easily recall that less than thirty years earlier I had spent four and a half years of my life in a conflict in which the country to which he felt such loyalty was, to put it as plainly as I know how, without naming any names, on the other side of the scrimmage line from our team.

Another thing that I believe, is that from a purely selfish standpoint, for every dollar that you spend in your home town or in your own country, a portion of it will eventually find its way back to you.

## Chapter XL

## THE GOOF-UP

It is never a pleasure to tell about your own mistakes, but sometimes it must be told because it is part of the story.

It was a busy time. We were doing a lot of business — one week alone we grossed a half million dollars. A large part of this was casing and tubing. I took quite a few pipe orders at night, sometimes in the wee hours.

One night about 2: A.M. I received a call for a string of 4 1/2 inch casing. It needed to be delivered right away. I wasn't really wide awake. I called the pipe yard and ordered the casing. They would start loading immediately. But somehow I gave directions to have the casing delivered to the wrong location, a location belonging to the same company but that had been drilled to total depth, had already run the oil string and that would be getting a string of tubing that same day. After I had made the call I lay there in bed for about an hour and a half. Then it hit me what I had done. What a horrible mistake!

I called the pipe yard. The pipe had been loaded and was on its way — to the wrong location!

But I knew how the pipe trucks would be travelling. They would go up I-77 and the drivers would stop at a cafe at the Coshocton Exit for a cup of coffee. I would catch them there. When I went into the cafe they weren't there! My heart sank. But pretty soon the two drivers came in. I had beaten them there. I gave them the correct directions and the crisis was over.

# Chapter XLI

## THE OHIO OIL AND GAS ASSOCIATION MEETING

It was in late January of 1977. The Ohio Oil and Gas Association was having their Mid-Winter meeting in Columbus. This was a two day affair. Mr. John Rhodes, Vice-President in charge of sales in our Oklahoma City office, had flown out to Ohio the day before.

He wanted to attend the meeting but also wanted to call on some of our clients in West Virginia. We got out early the following day and headed for West Virginia. We had a good day and made a number of nice sales calls in Charleston and in Clarksburg. We got back to New Concord about 4:30 in the afternoon, then headed for Columbus, a distance of seventy miles, where we would spend the night.

Up to this point it had been a real nice day, weatherwise — cool, but sunny. But when we came within fifteen or twenty miles of Columbus it began to snow, and I do mean snow! There were real big flakes and in no time at all there was an accumulation of several inches. And about eight miles from downtown Columbus the traffic jam began. At that point in time it was about 5:30. We put our car in number two forward gear and crept along, like maybe ten or fifteen miles per hour, then stop for a few minutes. Then maybe the traffic would move a couple of hundred yards and stop again. This routine was repeated for I'm sure dozens of times. We arrived at the hotel where the meeting was being held at 8:30 that night! It had taken us three hours to cover a distance of eight miles.

## Chapter XLII

## BUCKEYE SUPPLY COMPANY

Shortly after my arrival in New Concord, Ohio, I went over to Zanesville with one of the men who worked in Republic's store to sort of learn my way around. One of our stops in Zanesville was Buckeye Supply Company's store. While there I was chatting with one of the Buckeye men, a fellow by the name of Al Wesbar. He could tell that I was interested in their operations, so he volunteered to give me a guided tour of their place. First he showed me around their store, which was pretty impressive. They had a very well stocked store. Then he took me upstairs where their offices were located. It was a Saturday so most of the offices were not in use, but he told me what each office was for and who used it. Then he pointed out another office. The door was open, but he said it was not used anymore. It had belonged to Mr. B. Robert Straker, founder of the company, who had died a year earlier. This office was treated as s shrine of sorts to his memory. Several years later I was told one of his sons and President of the company, Charles Straker, had started using it again.

Founded in 1929, in Zanesville, a second store was opened in Wooster, Ohio in 1943. As time moved on other stores were opened and today Buckeye has seven locations in Ohio, Pennsylvania and New York.

Sure, they were competitors, but I couldn't escape being impressed. I was in the presence of an institution. I felt a sense of history here. Later, I was told that Buckeye was the grand-daddy, as it were, of the supply companies in Ohio. Many of the other companies were founded by former employees of Buckeye.

98

While I was in Ohio I became friends with several of their employees: the Strakers, Don Long, Dick Gutridge, Bearcat Barrick, Al Wesbar, and I'm sure some others that I can't bring to mind at the moment.

During my six years in Ohio I always felt that these people were governed by the best ethical business principles.

## Chapter XLIII

## EARLY RETIREMENT AND BACK TO KERMIT

In February of 1979 I retired from Republic Supply Company. It was voluntary early retirement (I was 63) but I had worked 33 years for them. I had decided a year or two earlier that I had seen enough of the oil field and that I wanted to finish writing my books and when not doing that I would golf and fish. I had given Republic what I considered adequate notice — something like six months.

I retired in Ohio, but as might be expected, I moved bact to Texas to live. After all, when I moved to Ohio six years earlier, I had kept my home, furniture and other property and as stated before, it was my full intention to move back there, sooner or later.

The first month after retirement was just like a long vacation. When I started to get up in the morning I would say: 'Wait a minute, you don't need to hurry, you're retired.''

But in the second month I began to get restless. As the saying goes I was getting to the point where I was about ready to climb a wall. I began to realize that I wasn't quite ready to divorce myself from the oil field or from work, either. My brother Holt, who lived in Midland, Texas, was a manufacturer's representative. He was twelve years older than me. His trade territory was pretty big —

*The Author Shortly After Retirement From Republic in 1979*

all of West Texas and Southeast New Mexico — and he
needed some help. Prior to my retirement from Republic I
had agreed to help him, like maybe one week a month.
For compensation we agreed that he should pay me $290
per month, which was the maximum I could draw at that
point in time and still draw social security, plus mileage
on my auto and any other expenses incidental to my sales
efforts.

This arrangement worked pretty good for a while. I
certainly had no complaint as far as Holt was concerned,
but pretty soon I became increasingly restless. Let's face
it! I was missing the challenge of the supply business.

Of course there were challenges in Holt's business too,
but I hadn't gotten adjusted to it and into the swing of
things. I was in a state of limbo. I was wishing that I
hadn't retired from Republic.

I had maintained contact with the Company and, in fact,

had suggested to Jerry Bergin, their Executive Vice-President, that I might be available for something, if needed. Then, in July 1979, Jerry called me. The store manager of their store at Oak Hill, West Virginia had quit. They were in a bind. I was familiar with the store and its operation. In fact I had directed its inception two years earlier, when I was District Manager for the area. Would I come out of retirement and help them for say, three months, on a contract or consulting basis, to bridge the gap, so to speak, and regroup? I agreed to do so and in late July, 1979, I drove to West Virginia.

Holt and his wife, Jessie May, were less than jubilant about this. To them I had gone back to Republic Supply Company and his dream of working me into his business had been blown. I must confess that it looked that way.

In September we had a family reunion at Hot Springs, Arkansas. I flew down there from West Virginia. It was perhaps one of our better reunions. But it was to be the last one at which all of my brothers and sisters and myself would attend. As we parted on that last morning of the reunion I saw something in Holt and Jessie May's eyes that I didn't recognize for what it was at the time— that this was probably the last time that he and I would see each other in this life. How prophetic it was to be!

A month later, I drove back to West Texas from West Virginia. I felt that I had done my job for Republic. I think they did too, but I was glad to get back. I believe that I had gotten Republic Supply Company out of my system. I drove up to the Holt McWorkman residence. I was tired. I was looking forward to having a drink with Holt. Jessie May met me at the door. Holt had had a very serious heart attack the night before. He was in the hospital. The prospects were not good. He died within an hour after I arrived in Midland.

It was a Thursday. On the Saturday following we had

planned to attend the Permian Basin Pioneer's meeting and dinner, which meets every odd numbered year in Midland. Of course this was not to be.

I have, you might say, sort of dragged you into my own emotional experiences. I do not consider this as unnecessary. Holt was a part, I think, and a typical part of the Permian Basin oil scene, of the oil field, per se. He was not oil field trash. He drank, but he did not neglect his family. He was a good salesman, and a creative one, who contributed to the improvement of products and services offered to the oil industry. This is not only the spirit of the oil industry, but of the American Free Enterprise system as well.

A few weeks after Holt died, Fowler Gilchrist, the president of Clow Corportaion, for whom Holt had been the sales representative, called me and asked if I would try to carry on where Holt had left off. I said that I would. I represented them for five and a half years. Then I hung it up for good as far as my selling career was concerned.

## Chapter XLIV

## THE BOOM

But let us continue.  Brother Holt would have been surprised at some of the things that have happened in the oil fields since he died in 1979.  The next two years would see things happening that neither I nor any other living person had ever witnessed and most likely never will again.  The oil field went wild!

The energy crisis of 1973, precipitated by the Arab Embargo and the OPEC increases in the price of crude oil in the 1970's had already stimulated a lot of activity in the exploration phase of the petroleum industry.  In the 1980 presidential election Ronald Reagan defeated Jimmie Carter.  One of the first things Reagan did after being inaugurated was to decontrol the price of crude oil.  This set things off.

In 1981 there were more rotary drilling rigs (over 4,800) in operation in the United States than there had ever been before.  Unfortunately, some of these rigs should never have been in operation — some of them were pure junk! The personnel on many of the rigs was also less than adequate.   There were drilling superintendents that weren't qualified toolpushers, toolpushers who weren't good drillers, drillers that weren't even good roughnecks and roughnecks — well, some of them should have stayed at the house! "Warm bodies" were working on drilling rigs — they were also working on well servicing units.

Because of this lack of experience on drilling rigs, there was a period in which "consultants" were in big demand. What this amounted to was that because of the shortage of experience on drilling rigs, people who did have the experience and know-how could be used as needed in time of crisis such as lost circulation problems, blowouts, fishing jobs, and so on. These people were hired on a daily basis and they were paid pretty good, from $300 to $500 per day. That sounds pretty rich, but after all, when you are drilling a well that will cost as much as a million or so, what's $500 a day for expert advice? Of course, like the rest of the industry, there were some consultants who weren't really qualified, either.

I was told of one fellow who served as a consultant on well completions. He made pretty good money, too — two or three hundred a day. But he spent it as fast as he made it, and when the boom collapsed he had to hitch-hike the four hundred miles back to his home in West Texas.

During the boom, money flowed like wine. There was a lot of wheeling and dealing. I was told of one instance when four fellows sat at a table in a cafe. As the story goes, when they had finished their dinner they left a fifty dollar tip on the table for the waitress!

One of the sadder things in all of this is that a number of people went into the drilling business who shouldn't have. With some of them their eventual failure might be attributed to hard luck. But many of them just didn't know what they were doing! Some of them didn't even know all of the mechanics of drilling an oil well. And a whole bunch of them weren't business men; and didn't recognize the fact that if you financed your operation with twenty percent money, you just couldn't have any hard luck, that all of your receivables had better pay off on time and that the boom in the oil field held. Which it didn't!

This idiocy extended beyond the drilling phase of the industry, to the oil field supply stores and to some manufacturing. Prior to the boom there were eight manufacturers of oil field pumping units. At the height of the boom more than two hundred had gotten into the act. Though perhaps not to such a dramatic extent, the manufacturing of sucker rods was similarly affected. In what I would call the "general" oil field supply business there were a number of newcomers. Like in the drilling rig end of it, some of them just shouldn't have gotten into it. Then there were expansions and openings of new stores by the older companies like National Supply Company, Continental-Emsco Company, Oilwell Division of U.S. Steel, The Bovaird Supply Company, and Republic Supply Company. Of course these latter companies managed to survive, but they didn't expect what would happen in 1982 and they were all hurt by it. They knew, of course, that the boom wouldn't last forever, but they didn't expect it to come to an end so suddenly. 1981 was a very busy year, the busiest the oil field had ever experienced. Sure, we had seen booms before, but they had been confined to certain fields or areas like Burkburnett, Borger, Seminole, Wink and others, but never before had it boomed all over the oil field at once!

During the boom of 1980 and 1981 there was a tremendous demand for walking beam type pumping units, a demand that the traditional manufacturers — who numbered less than a dozen — just couldn't meet. It seemed to be too good an opportunity to pass up and as earlier stated, at one time there were over two hundred manufacturers of these units. Quite a few of these units were, to put it charitably, not sufficiently engineered. Some stayed in operation only a few months. But, in a sense, they served a good purpose. I think that quite a few of the oil operators knew that were taking a gamble and that these eleventh hour units wouldn't last, but it did enable them to buy some time and produce some oil while the price was up, against the day when they could obtain more dependable equipment. Of course, when the slowdown came in 1982, most of these two hundred or so newcomers disappeared from the scene, many of them in one form of bankruptcy or another.

Most informed predictions were that the boom would last perhaps for five years and would likely taper off back to normal during the last year or so of that period.

## Chapter XLV

## THE BUST AND THE AFTERSHOCKS

But in early 1982 it happened. The boom came to a screeching halt. It was as though it was controlled by a valve that was suddenly closed. I have mentioned drilling contractors, well servicing companies, supply companies and manufacturers as being participants in, and later victims of, the boom. Oil companies were not exempt, either, particularly those who had borrowed high priced money and plunged heavily into some programs, some of them not too well thought out.

But there were some who deserved to succeed, and would have, I believe, had the boom held for another couple of years. I had a couple of friends who went into the supply business. They were good, hard working, experienced supply men. They weren't wheeler-dealers. They just didn't have enough time in which to make it. I haven't heard from them in several years, but I think both of them are of the caliber that they will bounce back, if they haven't already done so.

During the boom of 1981, the economy of the oil field, including West Texas and Southeastern New Mexico, was so different from that in the other parts of the United States that it was as though we were in two different countries. We were in an economic boom, the rest of the country in a recession. Partly because of the increase in the price of crude oil, the country as a whole was experiencing double digit inflation and during that time interest rates were also very high, the highest we had ever seen, which had a depressing effect on much of the economy. Of course, the high price of crude oil was the main source of the prosperity in the oil field.

And for those who had saved any money and could get in on the money markets and certificates of deposit, it was a great opportunity. I was fortunate enough to get a few thousand dollars in CD's that paid above sixteen percent. For those who had a lot of money it was a chance to get even richer.

But for those who went into business during this period of time and borrowed eighteen or twenty percent money, well, that is another story. Frankly, even if the boom had held for another three years, I seriously question whether or not a business operating with twenty percent money could have succeeded. All conditions would have had to have been almost perfect. Take the case of an oil field supply company. First, the management would have had to be beyond reproach, which would have meant a high level of efficiency and good personnel throughout. Operating on high priced money, good inventory control and a high rate of inventory turnover would be a must. Credit would be critical, too. You just couldn't afford to have any bad receivables. And in times of high interest rates even the good credit risks are inclined to drag their feet when paying their invoices, which means, in effect, that they will use your money as long as they can. And finally, the percentages of gross profit that you are able to keep is very important. If you have given up any sizeable percentage of your profit in order to do business with an account, they had better be very good pay and you had better have a good inventory turnover. While the factors involved are somewhat different for a drilling contractor

**107**

or a well servicing company, the basics are the same. Return on investment is the key.

During the boom the demand for materials and services was so great that it was a "seller's market". Indeed, there are people who say that some suppliers of services and materials took advantage of the oil companies, and have suggested that this was one of the reasons behind the slowdown in activity, that the oil companies deliberately slowed things down. This might have been a factor but I think pure economics was probably the main cause.

Because of the dramatic increase in the price of crude oil by the OPEC countries, which, of course, was reflected in the price of gasoline at the pump and in the price of fuel oil, a widespread effort at conservation resulted. This coupled with a worldwide recession in industry in 1981 and 1982, brought about a marked reduction in the consumption of energy. A glut of crude oil and a reduction in the price of crude oil resulted. Instead of $38.00 per barrel we were now talking about $28.00 When this happened the oil operators drilled fewer wells, and when they did they asked the drilling contractor, the oil well servicing people and the supply companies to sharpen their pencils. What had been a seller's market in 1981 became a buyer's market in 1982.

I have previously referred to the need for a good inventory turnover in the case of the supply companies. This would translate into high percentage use of equipment in the case of the drilling contractors and service companies. I have also referred to the need for maximum profit percentages and for good receivables in the face of high priced money. In 1982 all of these desirable conditions collapsed. There was absolutely no way that companies who had borrowed twenty percent or higher money in 1980 or 1981 to go into oil related businesses could survive, unless they had been favored with all of the ideal conditions above mentioned.

A number of drilling contractors, oil field supply companies, manufacurers and other classifications went into bankruptcy, the most common of which is known as Chapter 11. Even banks failed!

The old time companies in the oil field related segments of the economy survived. They had the advantage of having a large part of their inventory and/or equipment paid for and of having the previous experience of several boom-bust cycles under their belt. But even the old timers were hurting for a while. A lot of companies reduced — or froze — their employees' salaries and adopted programs of austerity in general. Of course, for oil companies who had not found it necssary to borrow high interest money and who had oil production before the price of crude went up, these people did alright. I had several independent oil company friends who were struggling back in the 1960's. When the price of oil went up, they "got well" as the saying goes. and I was glad to see it happen to them.

The sad thing about all of this was that a lot of good people got hurt. The guy or gal between twenty and thirty years old who had made a mistake had time to regroup and start over, but for the people in their fifties who did so, it was a little late to start all over and it was pretty disheartening with kids still in college.

The banks that failed were for the most part those whose loans were energy oriented or made to real estate or other ventures in areas dependent upon the energy industry. While fraud was involved in some cases, bad judgment and unforeseen circumstances were probably the main reason for these failures. And quite likely this bad judgment was influenced a great deal by the high rate of return on these loans.

The failure of many businesses came about from the chain reactions. If an oil company didn't pay the drilling contractor, the drilling contractor couldn't pay the bank or the supply company, the supply company had problems meeting their obligations and so on down the line. When you are operating with high interest money you just can't have a cash flow problem.

But the old heads knew that the oil field would come back. Not to the almost ridiculous pace of 1981, but to a more normal, sensible situation where people in all phases of the business could, with good management, hope to realize a respectable profit.

# Chapter XLVI

## A MATTER OF ECONOMICS AND NATIONAL SECURITY

It is now 1985. There is still some fallout from the bust that hit the oil field in 1982. Companies are still taking Chapter 11 and Chapter 7 bankruptcies and banks are still failing. And the domestic oil industry has not recovered as well as we had hoped.

There are several reasons for this. For one thing, there is still a glut of oil and natural gas. The price of crude oil has been further depressed for that reason and there are even predictions that the price could even go as low as $20 a barrel. Another thing hurting all domestic industry is the strength of the U.S. dollar versus foreign currencies. It is thought that this is due in great part to our high interest rates. In any case, it backfires on us because it hurts our foreign trade balance. In fact, we are importing not only crude oil, but refined products as well.

Another restraining factor on domestic exploration for oil and gas are the proposals for tax reforms made late last year by the Treasury department when a fellow by the name of Regan was Secretary. Their proposals would not only eliminate the depletion allowance for independent oil and gas producers, but would do away with the deduction for tax purposes of intangible drilling costs. It will be necessary, of course, for the Congress and the President to pass on these proposals, but it has injected enough uncertainty into the picture that there are fewer rigs running now than there were a year ago.

As if to add insult to injury, Texas' own governor, Mark White, has proposed increasing the filing fees for drilling wells from $100 to $900. That doesn't sound like much, but when added to the other problems of the industry, it could represent the well known straw that broke the camel's back.

And, of course, none of us have forgotten the windfall profits tax.

It seems that just about everyone outside the industry are determined to make whipping-boys of the oil and gas operators, especially the independents.

Ironically, the people who will eventually suffer the most from such short-sighted policies will be the people who are in favor of them now, the big consumers in the non oil producing areas of our country, for in the absence of vigorous exploration for oil and gas we will be moving in the direction of greater dependence upon foreign sources for our energy. Some of these sources are not especially interested in our well-being, and, in fact, would delight in having us at their economic mercy, or worse.

What it all adds up to is this: Regardless of what Congress, or the President, or the Governor of Texas do, the law of supply and demand will eventually take over. But maybe instead, the OPEC countries will dictate the price of oil and in that instance the aforementioned entities will be powerless to do anything about it. This is not a pretty scenario, is it?

Just imagine! $2.00 a gallon (or more) for gasoline in present day real dollars, and, of course, a correspondingly higher price for many other things in which oil plays a part, either as raw material or as energy in producing it. We are talking about the lifeblood of our manufacturing, transportation, utilities, and yes, farming, too! And inflation! We thought we had seen some of it a few years ago, but if energy prices got out of our control, the prospect isn't pretty, is it?

Another thing that has come about in the past couple of years is the rash of takeovers and mergers. Some of them are good, I think, but a lot of them hurt the economic health of the oil industry, and parenthetically, a bunch of good working people as well. Some of the prime movers in these takeover have defended them as looking out for the best interest of the stockholders and bringing about leaner, better managed companies. Some make no apologies, simply saying that there's nothing wrong with making money, you know, the old Free Enterprise system.

Concerning the first argument, a merger that will allow the resources, expertise and management skills of two companies to complement each other, resulting in a stronger corporate entity, can be good, and can be a productive thing for the industry. But mergers or takeovers done strictly to make a profit on the transaction itself, particularly the hostile takeovers, sometimes referred to as "greenmail", are a bad thing. Not only does it disrupt the organization being taken over — often with resulting losses of jobs for employees — but it ties up investment capital that could be used for more benign and productive purposes. In other words, like a poker game or a lottery, it doesn't produce anything.

As to the second line of thinking, I can only say that there are a lot of ways of making money, some of them pretty unsavory, like prostitution and pornography. "Making money" is not the sole answer to the American Free Enterprise system. If the present trend of mergers was to continue to its ultimate conclusion, the end result would be that there would be only two classes of businesses: the mega corporations, that no one could touch, and the very small companies. The medium sized companies that would need to go on the stock market to secure capital would be eliminated. I don't think that this is a healthy prospect for the oil and gas industry or for the economy in general.

There is no question in my mind that the oil and gas industry will survive. But there could be some rough times ahead for them, and in time, for the consumer as well.

What I am saying is that the law of supply and demand will eventually assert itself. The price of fossil energy will eventually go up, partly because of increased demand and partly because of an inadequacy of supply. The increase in prices will provide the incentive to search for more reserves, to produce energy from sources like shale oil, tar sands and coal gasification, that currently are not economically feasible. Also, when the price gets high enough, there will be justification for the use of some methods of secondary and tertiary receovery of the oil still in place in our existing fields, that are not currently feasible.

The more serious aspect of the problem is one of national security. We simply cannot allow ourselves to be dependent on OPEC oil. Our President and Congress must provide an economic climate that encourages the search for new reserves. Also, something needs to be done to discourage green-mail hostile takeovers that divert investment capital from more productive uses.

An aspect of imports of crude oil and refined products that is sometimes overlooked is what it does to our balance of payments picture. It has been estimated that oil imports acount for about half of our trade deficit. It should be remembered, too, that our economic wellbeing is also a measure of our national security.

As you have probably noticed, this is being written over a period of several years. It is now late February in 1986. Since the first of the year, the price of crude oil has dropped dramatically, from something like $27.00 a barrel to $15.00 and it is still moving down. Some economists say that this is good for the economy of the country as a whole, on the basis that cheaper energy will reduce the cost of manufactured goods, our cost of living and our foreign trade deficit. I will agree with this line of thinking, as far as it goes. But what about the oil producing third world countries that owe our banks, who were already having a problem paying just the interest on those debts? And what about our oil producing industry? Hundreds of thousands of jobs are endangered by the reduced activity that this will bring about: reduced drilling, reduced production, transportation, refining of petroleum and, of course, the functions of those other people who attend to the needs of the people directly involved in the industry. In the Permian Basin alone there are already numerous layoffs and even closings of businesses and the end isn't in sight.

But of importance to our country as a whole, the reduction in our exploration for oil will later lead to a further decline in our already declining reserves of oil and gas and a greater dependence upon imported oil. This would not only reflect in larger trade deficits, but endanger our national security as well.

Someone has said that we could go back to the prices of crude oil that prevailed in 1972 — around $3.25 a barrel for West Texas intermediate crude — if everything else was rolled back to that level, too, but of course, there is no way that will ever happen. Wages and materials used in the exploration for and production of oil can never be moved back to that level, although the competitive situation has caused some adjustments to be made in those respects.

As earlier stated the ratio of success versus failure in drilling wildcat or exploratory wells is about one in six. Unfortunately, the successes, the gushers, make the headlines, the dry holes do not. Another fact that is not always recognized is that every oil and gas well will eventually exhaust its potential. The time involved will vary, of course, but in due time any given well will cease to produce. Of course, secondary — and perhaps later, tertiary — recovery may extend the life of the well. But fossil fuels are an exhaustible source of energy!

## Chapter XLVII

## A CHANGE OF SCHEDULE

When I was a travelling salesman in the last five and a half years of my career, I always tried to maintain a schedule. I had my itinerary for at least one week already planned. Indeed, my entire five or six week circuit was pretty well mapped out. But even the best laid schedules can go awry. Such was the case in the incident that I am about to relate.

For a number of years I have suffered, on occasion, from muscle spasms in my lower back area. For those of you who have never experienced this problem, it can be a very painful thing. I have, in fact, said that if I had to put up with it from now on, that I would "sell out pretty cheap".

On one of my trips to Abilene, Texas, I felt when I left home that I might have a seizure coming on. You learn to sense something like this. I had also found that these seizures would often come on when I had been working long hours and sometimes when I had been under quite a bit of tension or stress.

On my trips to Abilene I usually figured on it being a three-day thing. I would work my way to Abilene, making calls at Big Spring, Westbrook, Sweetwater and Merkel and arrive in Abilene between 4:00 and 5:00 in the afternoon. I would then check in at the Colonial Inn Motel for two nights. On the following day I would work my

116

clients in the city of Abilene. On the third day I would work Ranger, Eastland, Cisco, Albany and then head for home.

I realized on this trip that I might be faced with some problems with my back, but thought a good night's sleep might straighten it out. I can say that I am not a hypochondriac and I really have to be sick for anything to keep me from going.

The next morning I got out of bed. I was combing my hair in front of the mirror. Then one of those spasms hit me. I broke out in a cold sweat and went to my knees! I decided right then that this sales trip was over. I called the desk and told them I was checking out. I got one of the chambermaids to help me get my things in my car. After checking out I drove directly to Kermit. And upon arriving home I went directly to my Doctor's office to get one of those sonic wave treatments that his nurse gave me when I had one of these seizures. The first treatment helped a lot, but it took two more to really straighten me out.

## Chapter XLVIII

## OUT OF TOWN SELLING

In the first thirty years of my time in the business, I did very little out-of-town overnight travelling and selling. When I did start doing this type of selling, I soon found that things are quite a bit different than when you are at home base every night. For one thing, you have to be better prepared, to have your act together better, so to speak. You can't run back to the office for a catalog on short notice. Also, since your out-of-town calls are less frequent for the most part than your calls at home, you need to say everything that needs to be said, to touch all bases, as it were, for it might be quite a while before you see your client again.

Even making sure you have all of your personal belongings with you that you need on a trip can be a problem. One time I had driven a few miles from home and noticed that I had failed to bring along my book with all the names and addresses in it. I had no choice but to go back and get it, as I would have been, perhaps not helpless, most certainly handicapped, without it. One time I drove to Abilene where I would spend two nights. Upon checking into my motel room I discovered that I had left my hangup clothes at home. The following morning I went to a drygoods store and purchased a shirt and a pair of trousers to get me by.

On one of my trips to Levelland, Texas, where I always spent one night, upon returning to my home the following afternoon, I discovered that I had left my hangup clothes in my motel room in Levelland. I called the motel. The people there took care of my clothes until I was able to get back up there a few weeks later. Some of my friends suggested that I might have had to leave Levelland in a hurry, and under pressure!

When I went to Artesia, New Mexico, I almost always spent the night. On one of these trips — upon checking into the motel I discovered that I had left my suitcase at home. This had my clean underwear, socks, shaving gear and other toilet articles in it. The clothing stores were closed by the time I had made the discovery, but I went to a supermarket and bought a throw-away razor, toothbrush, toothpaste, shaving lotion and so on. After I had eaten supper and returned to my room, I undressed, washed my underclothes and socks and stood in front of an open space heater in my birthday suit drying them.

To prevent such predicaments from happening, my brother Holt and some other salesmen I have known, had a briefcase packed with a few toilet articles, a pair of socks, a handkerchief and a set of undies. This they left in

118

their car at all times. In addition to meeting the above described emergencies, it came in handy when they were detained overnight unexpectedly. On a normal trip they packed their suitcase as though this briefcase wasn't there.

A few incidents such as the above taught me to do a "double-take", not only when leaving home for a trip, but when checking out of a motel as well.

And sometimes money can become a problem. While I was in Ohio with Republic Supply Company, I had to make several trips to Rochester, New York, as we had a customer doing some exploratory work in the Finger Lakes area just south of that city. In those days I stayed for the most part in Holiday Inns. I did this for several reasons. Besides being first-class motels, at that point in time, I could use my Gulf Oil Company courtesy card for lodging, food and drink when staying there. It wasn't that I was all that broke, it simply meant that I didn't need to worry about carrying a lot of cash on me.

On my last trip to Rochester I discovered upon my arrival there that there had been a fire at the Holiday Inn at which I had been staying and it would be months before they would be back in operation. There was a Sheraton Inn nearby, so I went there and checked in. It was my plan to spend only one night in Rochester and I had plenty of cash in my billfold to handle that, as well as my other expenses, but not much more.

Then, as sometimes happens in the selling business, my plans were altered. The man I needed to see was not immediately available so I had to stay over another night. As I was more than four hundred miles from home it didn't make any sense going home and then coming back. I explained my problem to the people in the Sheraton. By skipping dinner and drinks I had enough to bail myself out in the morning. I did not have a Master or Visa or

American Express Card at that point in time. I did have a pocket full of various oil company courtesy cards. No, they couldn't take any of them. I could give them a check on my bank account in New Concord, Ohio. No Way! But go ahead and have dinner and drinks. I could call my bank in the morning, get confirmed and then pay them by check.

The next morning I arose and had breakfast. Shortly after I returned to my room from the coffee shop, the phone rang. I picked up the receiver, but there was no one on the other end. A little later there was a knock on the door. It was a very well dressed, nice looking young lady. She said she was just the maid checking rooms. If she was a chambermaid, I'll eat my golf cap! Besides 8:00 A.M. is a little early to be checking rooms. No, what they were doing was checking on me, making sure I hadn't taken off without paying my bill!

I was virtually a prisoner in my motel room. This irritated me. If my intentions had been to beat my motel bill, why would I have levelled with them the evening before? Also, if those had been my intentions, I could have left about four in the morning and been a long way down the road by getting up time.

I called my bank in New Concord, Ohio at 9:00 and had my personal check approved. I then wrote a check for the entire bill.

It taught me one thing, however. If any extensive traveling is contemplated, whether personal or on business, everyone needs some kind of back-up in the form of a courtesy card that is pretty well universally accepted. You just can't carry enough cash or traveler's checks for every eventuality, or at least it isn't practical to do so. I now carry one of these cards at all times. I use it every once in a while, whether I need it or not, just to be sure it stays active.

## Chapter XLIX

## SOME OIL FIELD NICKNAMES

When I came to the oil fields in 1946, there were a lot of oil field nicknames, more so, I think, than is now the case. I will name a few of them: Toolbox Jones, Pig Iron Smith, Baroid Harrod, Oil Can Pugh, Onion Dennis, Buttermilk Dennis, and a fellow called Stick Horse (I can't recall his last name). Then there was Eight Ball, Lightning, Speedy, Too Tall, Cotton, Peewee and Peanuts. In Artesia there was Static Collier and Junky Jenkins. And of course there was Jelly Ellis, the District Manager in West Texas for Republic Supply Company and for whom I worked for something like fifteen years. There was an excellent gentleman named Froggy Vogle, who sold, among other things, steam traps. And there was Blue Watson, a barber frend of mine in Hobbs and his son, Rip. And Blue Eyes Clark, of Phillips Petroleum Company in Odessa.

Brother Holt's nickname was Box and Pin. This was derived from the fact that in his earlier years he was a sucker rod salesman and sold box and pin sucker rods.

My nickname was "Bull Plug". I'll never know why I was given that name. But a nickname is an asset to a salesman. People would remember Bull Plug when they wouldn't remember Lee.

And while this does not involve a nickname, somehow all of this reminds me of a travelling salesman from San Angelo who sold tailor-made suits. His name was Bob Ward. The signs on the sides of his car said: "Bob Ward has fits." I bought a suit from him and it fit perfectly.

## Chapter L

## PUTTING THINGS IN PERSPECTIVE

The following concerns a production foreman for one of the major oil companies. The time involved was the late 40's or early 50's. He was an old timer, of the old school, and had come up the hard way.

A young reservoir engineer had determined that a certain well in the Kermit area should have a hydraulic fracturing treatment. Further, it was his idea that this should be done on a given weekend, and he made it known to the production foreman that he expected it to be done at that time.

But Monday morning came and the frac job had not been performed. This disturbed the young engineer greatly and he made his displeasure known, not only to the foreman, but to others higher up in the organization, indeed, even to the home office level. In answer to the resulting questions the foreman wrote a letter that I consider classic in the way it puts things into their proper perspective. In substance it said: "I am told by our geologist that the oil in the formation to be treated has been in place for approximately 150 million years. That being the case, I didn't figure a couple more days would make that much difference."

## Chapter LI

## AN OFFICE TO REMEMBER

Mr. Roy Carter was superintendent of Carter Foundation Production Company's operations in West Texas and Southeastern New Mexico. Not only were he and his company good customers of Republic Supply Company, but I considered him a good personal friend as well.

But this is about Mr. Carter's office, which was a classic in itself, and which perhaps in some manner reflected the personality of its occupant.

The first things that met the eye of a visitor to Mr. Carter's office were papers, stacks of them, on his desk, on another table and on the floor. There were literally thousands of them: invoices, delivery tickets, pamphlets from manufacturers, quotations, you just about name it, they were there.

Now, this apparent jungle of paper was no accident, no result of his inefficiency or laziness. To him there was no disarray. This was the way he wanted it to be. And I was told that if he needed a particular document he could unerringly reach out and take it from one of the stacks of papers.

During the several years in which I made visits to his office I was a cigarette smoker. But you can be sure that I never smoked while I was in his office — a stray spark or a hot coal from a cigarette would have been sheer disaster.

A salesman who had never been in his office before made the remark — I suppose for lack of anythng better to say — that his office would be a good place for a fire. This comment went over with Mr. Carter about like the proverbial lead balloon. On another occasion, a visitor to his office suggested that he was in bad need of a secretary. He assured his visitor that he had no problem in that respect, and gave the impression that if he needed advice along that line he would ask for it.

Someone told me that Amon G. Carter, Sr. (Roy Carter's halfbrother) founder and publisher of the Ft. Worth Star-Telegram, philanthropist and founder of the oil company that bears his name, kept an office quite like Roy did and that this was perhaps the inspiration for Roy to do likewise.

I am indebted to Mr. Dale Hoopes, superintendent for Carter Foundation for West Texas and Southeast New Mexico, for the accompanying photo of the late Mr. Carter in his office, taken sometime in the 1960's.

And speaking of Mr. Roy Carter, I am reminded of a story that he related to me about a tornado that occured in East Texas, around Kilgore, I believe.

As was typical in the old days, just about every farm house in the area had a large cast iron pot. I would guess that it would be at least ten gallons in capacity. These pots were used to wash clothes, render lard and make soap. They stood on integral legs that were perhaps three or four inches in height. For heat a wood fire would be built underneath the pot.

Came the day of the tornado. It did a lot of damage and among the unusual things that it did, it turned one of the big cast iron pots inside out. That is, the legs were then on the inside of the pot.

Mr. Carter told me that he realized that it was hard to believe this occurrence, but that he was living in the community at the time and he saw the pot with his own eyes.

*Mr. Roy Carter in His Office.* [*Photo circa 1960's*]

## Chapter LII

## TO STIMULATE A WELL

On the left side of Highway 115, the road that goes from Kermit to Wink and beyond, about three miles from Wink, and not too far from the "Wink Sink", Mallard Petroleum Company had an oil well. It was a pumper and I guess it had been a fairly profitable well through the years, but the owners decided to do some remedial work on it to the end that its production might be increased.

I don't know what all they did, but I'm sure they cleaned it out, maybe deepened it a little, might have hydro-fraced it. But whatever they did, it stimulated it. It began to flow oil and I do mean flow, lots of it!

Now, there were no valves on the casing or tubing to control this well. All the operators could do was bring in tanks, a bunch of them, to run the oil into. It might be said that they could have brought in people like Halliburton and killed the well, but I'm sure they didn't want to do that.

I have no precise figures on the production from this well, but was told that over a period of a few weeks it produced 50,000 barrels of oil.

In the meantime Humble Oil and Refining Company (now Exxon Corp.) had an old abandoned well about a half mile east of the Mallard well. They decided that they might as well get in on this bonanza. Their well had been abandoned for so long that it was covered up with six feet or so of sand. They had to get a surveyor to locate it and then had to dig down to the old well head. They went into this old well with the hope that they might get some of the lush production that Mallard had gotten. But all they got was saltwater and it was the end of the big production from the Mallard well, too.

## Chapter LIII

## SELLING BY TELEPHONE, REACHING OUT

In my opinion there is no real substitute for eyeball to eyeball contact in dealing with people. This is true, whether you are selling yourself, a bushel of apples or an idea. I have known of companies who obtained wide area telephone service and thought that they could thereby reduce or eliminate their sales force in the field. "800" numbers are a good adjunct but by no means a substitute for the boys or girls on the firing line.

But some of our selling, for very practical reasons, must be done by telephone. The important thing to remember in this connection is that in telephone calls the elements of eye contact and a friendly smile are absent. To offset this we must compensate in other ways. We must project ourselves or, in the words of AT&T, "reach out".

I really don't feel that all that much magic is involved. Let's sum it up in a few words. When a customer calls, let the party on the other end of the line know you're glad he or she called. Then, don't overload them with a lot of bull, but do project yourself in such a way that you are communicating with them on the same wavelength. Above all, be friendly, and if a problem exists, be sympathetic. Be considerate of your customer's time. If he wants to talk a while, fine, but don't tie up too much of his time with your own conversation. I have known people whom I literally hated to call because I had such a hard time getting loose from them.

Even though most of the business with an account is conducted by telephone, it is always helpful for the telephone salesman to meet as many as possible of the clients face-to-face.

Concerning this latter, I am reminded of an experience that I had when I was living in Ohio. The territory served by our store was so large that, of necessity, a great deal of our business had to be transacted by phone. I talked to some of our customers on the phone for a number of times before I had the opportunity to meet them personally. One of these people was Bill Hawk, a pipe line contractor, at Dover, Ohio. Finally, I went by his office to meet him and his lady secretary. It so happened that they were both in the office. After introducing myself they both burst out laughing. Then they explained why. When we talk to someone on the phone whom we have never met, we visualize in minds-eye what the other person looks like. They had pictured me as very tall, sort of a John Wayne type. I stand five feet four and a half inches tall and weigh a hundred fifty-two pounds!

## Chapter LIV

### PRANKS IN A SUPPLY STORE

Through the years we had quite a few pranksters working in our stores. One prank that was pulled from time to time went like this. One of the store hands would pretend to call the superintendent of one of our good customers. He would go through the dialing process, but unbeknownst to the observer, would immediately break the circuit. Then the conversation on this end of the line would start: "Is this George Jones? This is Joe at Republic Supply Company. I understand you need some sucker rods." A pause. "When do you need them?" Another pause. "Tomorrow? No Way!" Another pause. "Well, if you don't like it, you can jump it!" Then he slams the receiver down.

The newer hands have been listening in utter disbelief. The store manager, if he is listening — and isn't in on the joke — is about to go into shock. A variation of the prank, and even more convincing, is to have a confederate call from down the street, then have a similar conversation as before.

What is to follow is supposed to have happened at Republic's Odessa store in the late 40's. One of the salesmen had left the store to go drink coffee with a customer. He left his briefcase on the store counter.

The briefcase contained some quotations and a number of items of descriptive literature concerning oil field items our compnay had for sale. While the salesman and his customer friend were gone, two of the boys in the store removed these items from the briefcase and replaced them with several sticks of lead babbitt metal. Each stick weighed about nine pounds.

When the salesman returned and picked up his briefcase, it almost jerked his arm off.

One day at our Kermit store the phone rang. One of our store employees, a real sharp young fellow, answered it. He talked for quite a while, at the same time doing a lot of writing on the order and rewrite pad. When he finally hung up the phone, he turned to me and said: "I just took a heck of a nice order. But now, what am I going to do with it?" I looked at the order. It was, indeed a nice one, but it was for mud products. The customer had reached the wrong number. He thought he was talking to Macgobar, a manufacturer of drilling muds and additives.

This one was told about a new hand at Republic's Odessa store. He had come to Odessa from a farming state like Iowa or Wisconsin and therefore had no previous knowledge of the oil field.

Ira Wells was the local representative for Oil Center Tool Company, who manufactured well heads of all kinds, including those large well head assemblies for deep wells known as Xmas trees.

When Mr. Wells came by the store, the young man greeted him and then asked him what he did. Ira said he sold Xmas trees. The young man observed that he supposed he was pretty busy in December, but wasn't business a little slow the rest of the year?

## Chapter LV

## NOT A MATTER OF SAVING MONEY

In the 1940's Mid-Continent Supply Company was a formidable competitor. In 1946 I think that there was little doubt that they were the Number One supply store in Kermit and I am sure that they were very strong at other points as well. Sometime in the late 40's or early 50's, Mid-Continent Supply Company put two-way radios in their field cars.

This was indicative, I think, of the business philosophy of Mr. K.W. Davis, founder and president of the company. One of his assistants asked: "Mr. Davis, how much money do you expect to save by putting these radios in your cars?" "We're not doing this to save money, we're doing it to make money!" was his reply.

## Chapter LVI

## DE-JA VU AND NOSTALGIA

When I was a travelling salesman it was inevitable that I would like to call on certain customers better than others. There were also certain places that appealed to me more than others. I am very fond of New Mexico, expecially Artesia. Every time I cross the New Mexico state line, a feeling of excitement possesses me. Don't ask me why! When you enter Lea County, New Mexico ten miles north of Kermit, it is not all that scenic. Of course, lest the reader get the wrong impression from what I have just said, there is much beautiful and exciting scenery in other parts of the state.

In the late forties and early fifties, I lived in New Mexico at Artesia and at Hobbs. Between the time I left there in 1955 and 1979, I had been to Hobbs only a few times and in the twenty-nine years since I had left Artesia I had been there only twice. When I started going back there in 1979, it gave me sort of an odd feeling. Notwithstanding, I always looked forward to my trips into New Mexico.

For about a year I had Breckenridge, Texas, on my itinerary and I had a good feeling about going there. When I first went to Kelly Supply Company there, I had the feeling that I had been there before. It was a feeling that I never shook and I always looked forward to going there. When I was in Ohio with Republic Supply Company, I had a similar deje vu feeling when I would go to Newark, Ohio.

## Chapter LVII

## THE PERMIAN BASIN PETROLEUM EXPOSITION
## IN ODESSA, TEXAS

This exposition, or oil show as it is usually referred to, is held every two years on the even numbered years, in late October. I don't think I have missed even one of them in the last thirty years. Even during the six years that I was in Ohio, I managed to fly down and take in at least part of the show.

In 1980 and again in 1982 it was my privilege to work in Clow-Vega's exhibitor's booth at the show. During the first two days of the show, which were primarily for oil people, there were men from Clow's home office and also from some of the other sales areas, working with me. But on the last two days of the show — open to the general public — these out of town people started thinning out and from about noon Friday until late Saturday afternoon I pretty much had it to myself.

But a young lady friend of mine, named Angie Diller, came to my rescue. She volunteered to help me operate the booth. This was really a big help to me, otherwise it was almost impossible for me to leave the booth for a cup of coffee or a sandwich or even to go to the restroom.

In 1982, on the last day of the show, which was Saturday, I was pretty well dressed up. I'm no Clark Gable, but it was my best and I guess I looked pretty sharp. And, in my own way, I was projecting myself, putting my best foot forward, if you will, in presenting myself and my company's wares to the thousands of people who passed our booth. I know I shook a hundred or so hands. And Angie was doing her part, too. While she was not too familiar with the technical aspects of our

*Brother Holt [right] and Odell Davis in Booth at Permian Basin Oil Show. [Sometime in the 1970's]*

exhibits, she made our visitors feel at home and managed to hold them until I could find time to talk to them, if I was otherwise tied up at the moment.

Then Angie tapped me on the arm. I turned to her to see what she needed. A little girl — nine or ten years old, I guess — was standing there in front of our booth. Angie said the little girl wanted to shake hands with me. I obliged her. I suppose she thought I was a pretty important person, and I guess I made her day. I know it made mine. In fact, of the hundreds, maybe thousands, of people that I made contact with during the four days of the show, she stands out as the most important.

This was one of the several memorable experiences associated with my career in the game of selling. Unfortunately, it is a fact of life that we do not always appreciate the significence of events at the time they are occurring. But I do remember most of these occasions, and I think, just about all of the people.

In this connection, I have had arguments, differences of opinion if you prefer, about how long people are remembered. My contention has been that worthwhile memories of people never die.

After I got home from the 1982 Oil Show, late Saturday afternoon, I had a feeling of a job well done, but I was tired. Perhaps more tired than I realized. I decided that I deserved a drink. It helped. So I had another, and still a third one. By this time I was pretty well relaxed, so relaxed that the divan and the other furniture were starting to move around. I went to bed. I awoke about 6:oo the next morning. I felt like a million dollars.

One time when I was making a call on one of the independent supply stores, the first person I saw there was a young man whom I had seen only once before. He said: "I'm sure glad to see you, I need to order some soap from you." "Well," I replied, "I'm sorry to disappoint you, but I don't sell soap.'" "Oh," he said, "I'm sorry, I remember what you do sell now, but you look just like the fellow we buy our soap from." When I left the place, I turned to the young fellow: "I wish I were selling soap today, but say, when you do see that fellow that sells soap, give him my regards, and my sympathy."

## Chapter LVIII

## THE WINK SINK

Earlier I mentioned the Wink Sink. This phenomenon has perhaps more often been called the Kermit Crater. Either designation might be acceptable as it is just off Highway 115 between Kermit and Wink, about five miles from Kermit and three miles from Wink.

It was first noticed by an employee of Harvard Construction Company, on the morning of June 3, 1980, who had gone to the site to check for a leak on a twenty-four inch water line belonging to Gulf Oil Corporation. When he first saw it, he estimated its size to be twenty feet wide by twenty feet long and about forty feet down to the water. In a matter of two hours it had grown to approximately one-hundred feet by one-hundred twenty feet.

In two weeks it had more or less stabilized at three hundred ninety six feet by three hundred twenty one feet. It was about thirty-five feet to the water and the depth of the water estimated at from sixty five to seventy five feet.

The twenty-four inch line had to be replaced, and several other big inch lines had to be rerouted. The Shell Pipe Line people were watching the sink hole very closely as they had a big tank farm only a quarter of a mile away.

One oil well nearby was plugged lest the sink hole extend and swallow it up.

I was told that a number of Wink residents were pretty nervous about the possible extension of the sink hole in the direction of Wink or perhaps the possible occurrence of others in the area. And well they might be as there was no certainty as to the cause of the phenomenon. Besides, Wink was closer to it than Kermit and also was more

*The Kermit Crater [or Wink Sink] [Photo courtesy Bill Beckham and The Winkler County News]*

nearly in the same area geologically. I was told that some Winkites concentrated their more valuable and irreplaceable possessions so that they could take off with them on short notice.

A number of theories were brought forth as to the cause of the sink, but perhaps the most plausible one was that a salt section at a depth of about eleven-hundred feet had washed out by natural and/or manmade means. Then the structure above it, being somewhat weak and in some places cavernous, simply collapsed into the void below it.

I am no geologist, but in thinking about the sink I cannot help but recall the many billions of barrels of oil and water produced from the Hendricks Reef, the aforementioned Mallard well, the Humble effort nearby and the two light earthquakes in Winkler County, one in the 60's and another in the 70's.

## Chapter LIX

### NO NUMBER THIRTEEN

When I went to Artesia, New Mexico, in the days when I was a travelling salesman, I usually spent the night there. There were just too many calls to be made at Loco Hills, Artesia, Carlsbad and Roswell to make them all in one day.

Most of the time I stayed at the West Winds Motel on the south side of Artesia on the road to Carlsbad. I usually called a day or two ahead of time and made a reservation there.

On this particular trip I arrived at the motel about 5:30 p.m. Central Time — 4:30 Mountain Time. I checked in and the lady at the desk gave me the key to Room Number 14.

The people at the motel had been redoing the numbers on the rooms and some of the numbers had not been replaced on the doors. There was no number 14, but there was a number on Room Number 12. So I tried the key in the second door to the right of Number 12. But the key wouldn't work. I went back to the office and told the lady there what my problem was. She said: "Number 14 is the one next to Number 12. There is no Number 13."

It was something I had never noticed before, that hotels and motels do not have rooms with the number 13. Likewise, multi-storied office buildings have no thirteenth floors.

I guess there are quite a few superstitious people. I must confess that I, too, would not have been real comfortable staying in Room Number 13.

While I was living in Ohio, my friend and fellow employee, Fred Watson, told me of a couple of things that would cause bad luck that I had never heard of before. One of them is to change a calendar ahead of time. That is, as an example, to tear off the November sheet before it is December. When you do that, something dire is almost certain to happen. The other item of bad luck is to rock an empty rocking chair. Very bad luck, indeed, as someone will die!

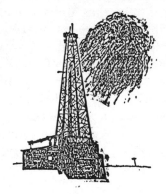

## Chapter LX

## NOT ON PRICE ALONE

When I was working for the supply company, I never chose to use price as a primary selling tool. Sometimes, of course, one is forced into a pricing situation. And, of course, it is nearly always necessary to be competitive. But I have never suggested to a customer that pricing would be the foremost factor involved. I have known salesmen whose standard approach was to ask if they could quote on something. What they were doing was, in effect, suggesting that they surrender some of their profit, profit from which their own salary and/or commission was derived!

One night, many years ago, I received a phone call from a good customer and friend — one of the two brothers who owned an independent oil company. He wanted the price of a certain size of pumping unit. I told him that I would check with the manufacturer and call him back, which I did in less than an hour. When he heard the price he blew his top. He had some choice remarks to make about the steel companies (Republic Steel Corporation was our parent company) and the pumping unit manufacturers. My reply was that our company had no control over the base price of the pumping units. I also said that our margin of profit was only ten percent and that if we couldn't make a decent profit there wasn't much point in making a sale. When we finished our telephone conversation he was still grumbling and said he would have to check and see. When I went to bed that night I really didn't know what to expect.

But at 6:30 the next morning he called me. He told me to get the pumping unit headed his way! What I had said to him the night before did make sense and did command his respect.

## Chapter LXI

## TRADEMARKS

I have heard people speak of the need for a person, particularly one in the selling business, to have a trademark of sorts. I even heard of one salesman who wore dirty clothes, which was that special something that people would remember him by.

One salesman friend of mine, Harry Denton, was remembered by the fact that he always handed his customers a cigar before he left their office or store. Others were remembered by their jokes. And some by their nicknames. The latter was the case with me. Early on in my career in the oil field supply business I picked up the nickname "Bull Plug". No special reason for it — except perhaps that I was a rather short person — it just happened. Many people remembered me by that name when they might have forgotten my given name, Lee.

While I think that these things can be assets, I feel that the important thing, rather than a trademark, per se, is that we have individuality and be our own person. We are all different and if we will be ourselves, that in itself is our trademark.

I worked thirty-three years for a sales organization and then five and a half years as a commission salesman for a manufacturer. But I spent the first several years literally fumbling around. My biggest problem during that period of time was that of establishing an identity. I was continually trying to be someone other than myself. Only when I started being my own person did I make any real progress. As I tell newcomers in the profession of selling, it is alright to borrow a page out of someone else's book, so to speak, to emulate certain of their qualities, but do not try to imitate them.

# Chapter LXII

## NOT STARVING TO DEATH

There are those who have said that a salesman should look hungry, to act like he needs the sale in order to have enough money for the next meal.

I believe that there is room for debate on this point. I realize that we all want to give the person just getting started in the business a little help, and sometimes we root for the underdog. And perhaps a salesman shouldn't be flashing a diamond stickpin or driving a Rolls Royce when making his calls. But on the other hand, I don't think people want to do business with a loser, either. I think they like the smell of success — maybe some of it will rub off on them. I think that this is especially true of salesmen who have been in the game for a number of years — customers like to think that they know what they are doing and feel that they deserve to be successful.

I have also been told not to use a new briefcase, that if it's real new it looks like you are real new in the game, too. Maybe there is something to that line of thinking, but I wouldn't want to carry a real shabby briefcase, either.

# Chapter LXIII

## SOME UNEXPECTED CHANGES

Change is in the essence of things, but some of the changes that have taken place in the last ten years are, to say the least, unexpected. If someone had suggested in 1972 that perhaps the biggest bank in the oilfield would ever be in trouble, he would have been laughed out of Midland. And who would ever have expected National Supply and Oil Well to merge? And I felt that there would always be a Republic Steel Corporation, whether or not the Supply Company survived. And who would have dreamed that Gulf would have been taken over by Chevron Oil or that Skelly would have merged into Getty and then the latter taken over by Texaco?

In the earlier years employees had a strong loyalty for the companies for whom they worked. They used to say that the old National Supply Company hands would be buried in blue coffins — National painted everything they had blue. I used to say that someone could bad-mouth me and maybe get away with it, but if they said anything about Republic Supply Company, those were fighting words. And there were a lot of other people who felt the same way about their company. The company was like family. But I am afraid that so many of the mergers and takeovers just previously discussed may have an adverse effect on this warm feeling toward one's employer.

Earlier in this discourse, at the time that I retired from Republic Supply Company, I said that, among other things I intended to do some golfing and fishing. For what it is worth, I think it should be noted that in the eight years since that time I have only golfed four or five times and as for fishing, I haven't wet a hook!

143

# Chapter LXIV

## ESPRIT DE CORPS

I think that it is time that I or somebody should say something about esprit de corps or company loyalty. It is pretty obvious that there has been a decline in old fashioned loyalty to company. Part of this decline has been due in part, I think, to the many mergers and takeovers that we have experienced in the past few years.

But I feel that loyalty to company is an important element of satisfying, productive employment. Once it has been established that an employee is a useful one for the company, and once the individual is convinced that he or she has become identified with a good reputable organization, I feel that absolute loyalty to that company is to be expected. And I also feel that this is a two-way thing, resulting in a somewhat family relationship between employer and employee, and between the employees themselves.

Concerning loyalty to company, I am reminded of a call I once made on Mr. Roy Carter, who at that time was superintendent for Carter Foundation Production Company for West Texas and Southeast New Mexico. On this call I was soliciting him for the casing for a well that they were about to drill. Mr. Carter said: "X X, Bull Plug, do you want all of my business?" I said: "Mr. Carter, quite frankly, I don't expect to get all of your business. Most of my competitors are my friends and they have my respect. But Republic Supply Company is paying my salary, and as long as they are doing so, I'm going to try and get all of your business that I can. The boys with those other companies can worry about their share of it." Incidentally, I think I made the sale, but in any instance, in the overall picture, Republic got the lion's share of their business.

While good ethics are desirable in the business world, most people do respect your loyalty and support for the company you are working for. Conversely, when a point is reached when an employee can no longer, in good conscience, give this loyalty and support to his company, I think it behooves that employee to cleanly terminate the relationship. My idea of a clean break is that notice of termination — at least two weeks — should be given, whether the termination be initiated by the employer or the employee.

How often have I heard the advice: "Sell yourself!" You must indeed project yourself, as it were, if you are to be successful in the profession of selling. But I feel that there is something more to be said in this respect.

When a company pays you a salary and/or commission, pays your expenses and furnishes you a car, thus providing you with an opportunity to make a living for yourself and your family, surely you owe that company something. Sure, when I was in the selling game, I wanted my clients to accept me, but I thought I owed it to the company for whom I worked, to give them a fair shake, too!

When I went to work for Republic Supply Company in 1946, I was an unknown quantity. In a sense I was a liability, as someone had to tell me how to do just about everything. The Company was paying my wages for me to learn about their business. The only way that they could realize any dividends on this investment was for me to stay with them after I had gotten my feet on the ground. I don't think I was an exception in this respect. I have known a number of rookie supply men who worked for a few months and began to show some promise. They hadn't "arrived" yet, but they did indicate some

145

potential. Some of them began to think they were underpaid and thought they should be managing the operation. And sometimes a competitor, noticing the possibilities in a new man, would entice him away from the company that had given him his bootcamp training, so to speak, by offering him more money. This happened to me several times when I was managing a store. In effect, we (my company and I) were proving out the potential and doing some of the training of personnel for a competitor. And doing it for nothing!

I have said that when I left the company for whom I worked so many years, whether it be retirement or some other way of termination, I would never go into direct competition with them, especially in the same area where I had been working. While this may seem a bit too much to expect of a former employee, I believe that there is a measure of rationale to justify this line of thinking. My thinking is that through the years I have been privy to certain company secrets that I would not otherwise have had access to. My sense of loyalty dictates that I not use this privileged information against my former employer.

No matter how good a company you may be working for and how much loyalty you may feel for that company, there will be times when you will become disenchanted or unhappy with your employer. The occasion that I am about to tell you about was one of those times. And thus it was that I attempted to call Charlie Hickman, one of the Vice-Presidents of Mid-Continent Supply Company.

Years earlier, in 1947, when Charlie was District Manager for that company in Kermit, he had told me that if I ever wanted to make a change, be it next month, next year, or ten years later, to give him a call. I was just a weevil (the oil field word for green hand) at the time, but I guess he must have seen some potential in me.

When I tried to call Charlie it was a weekend, so it was his residence phone number that I called. But there was no answer. I tried a number of times, but still no answer. He and his family must have been out of town for the weekend.

By Monday morning my dissatisfaction with my employer, Republic Supply Company, had cooled down. I never tried to call Charlie again. I will never know what the outcome might have been had I reached him on the phone that weekend.

## Chapter LXV

## "BULL DOG"

Whle she had nothing directly to do with the exploration for and the production of oil and gas, I feel that the little dog known as "Bull Dog" deserves a spot in this book.

This little dog was my constant companion for almost twelve years and also was almost a fixture at the Republic Supply Company store in Kermit, Texas during that same period of time. Indeed, when customers came into our store and didn't see her, they would ask where Bull Dog was.

J.L. Kingston, an employee of Republic, knew that I had been wanting to get a dog. I don't where he found her, but one winter morning in 1960, he brought her with him to the store in his coat pocket and handed her to me. She was just a little ball of fur at that point in time and couldn't have been over a week or two old.

She wasn't really a bull dog, but Rudy Holman, a long-time Republic employee, called her that when he first saw her and the name stuck. I don't know what breed of dog she was, but just about everyone who saw her said she looked more like a coyote than a dog. There were those who said she was probably half-coyote, but I have never confirmed whether or not that is biologically possible. As she grew older I thought that she paid particular attention when a coyote was serenading just outside our city limits, but maybe that was just my imagination.

I grew up in a tradition that held that dogs and cats were not to stay in a dwelling house, so except for a few days just after I had gotten her, she stayed in a little dog house that I had built for her. But later she just stayed out in the yard at night, rain or shine, snow, sleet or whatever.

She had a very heavy coat, consisting of more like sheep wool than hair. So cold weather never bothered her. One cold winter night she was sleeping out in the yard. It had snowed and sleeted, too. I heard her whining. I went out in the yard to see about her, as I figured the cold weather had finally gotten to her. But I found that that was not the problem at all. It was some dogs that were going down the street in front of the house that was disturbing her.

She wanted to go everywhere I went and if I drove off without her, she would run after the car. So I took her just about everywhere I went unless I was to be gone several days, like on vacation. And somehow, she always sensed when I was getting ready to take off on vacation. On the last two or three days before I left she wouldn't let me out of her sight. And she would whine a lot. Someone said that she probably thought I was leaving her for good and she would never see me again.

When I was at the store she would stay out in the showroom and quite often would take a nap. She would find the coolest place in the showroom, which was usually in a corner. But there was a peanut machine nearby and when someone clicked the lever on the machine she would immediately wake up and go over to the machine and beg for peanuts.

148

*"Bull Dog"* in Old Republic Store in Kermit

On weekday mornings we would have a few dozen doughnuts at the store for our customers. Some of them would give Bull Dog a doughnut from time to time. She dearly loved doughnuts, but she got as fat as a pig. I asked our customers not to give her so many of them, but she was still given too many. Finally, during the last year of her life, I kept her at home most of the time for that reason.

One time, when she was still pretty young, I had her in the house for some reason. I was eating a hamburger when the phone rang. I laid the hamburger on the kitchen table. While I was talking on the phone she got up on the table and took my hamburger. When I got through talking on the phone I didn't lay a hand on her, but I told her in no uncertain terms that I didn't appreciate her taking my hamburger, that it was my supper and I also reminded her that when she was eating her food she didn't appreciate anyone bothering her. Which was true. When she was eating she would growl if anyone — including me — came near her.

There is no doubt in my mind whatsoever that she understood everything I said. I think she may have cried a little. And I never had to worry about her taking my food again.

In early December of 1972, I went on vacation for something like ten days. When I returned from vacation I found that Bull Dog had died. I wasn't too surprised, as I had noticed for several months that she was beginning to show her age. After all, on the ratio of one year in the life of a dog being equal to seven of man, she was about seventy seven years old, a fairly ripe age. My good friend, Hugh Alexander, who watched after my house and fed her, too, when I was out of town, had buried her in my back yard.

150

## Chapter LXVI

## THE ROLE OF THE OIL FIELD SUPPLY COMPANY
## IN THE INDUSTRY

I think that a discussion of the oil field supply company, also known as a jobber, or middleman, and its place in the oil industry, is in order.

There are manufacturers and end users alike who think that "middleman" or jobber is a dirty word, that he is just someone who steps in between the manufacturer or producer and the end user and greedily grabs a share of the pie. To me this is an erroneous assumption and a gross injustice to the legitimate middleman or jobber.

Let us first explore the justification for there being a jobber from the standpoint of the end user or consumer. Number one: He eliminates the necessity for the consumer to maintain an inventory with the attendant cost of warehousing it. Ideally, the jobber will have most of the consumer's needs in stock, as they arise. Second: depending upon the type of merchandise being sold, a factor of service enters into the picture. This varies all the way from having the special needs of the customer in stock when he needs them, to those emergency situations when the jobber goes that extra mile and performs the seemingly impossible in getting his customer out of a bind. I could cite many examples of this kind of service: oil field supply men working all night or on Sundays or holidays, driving considerable distances, meeting planes at airports, whatever it took to keep the drilling rig or oil well operating. Number three: a source of specialized information on products and services that relieves the end user of the problem.

Now, what advantages are there, from the stand point of the manufacturer, in having jobbers, as opposed to selling direct? Again, there are several advantages. For one thing, jobbers eliminate the need for the manufacturer having field warehouses with large inventories, and, of course, personnel to man them. It also reduces the need for a large sales force in the field.

In the five and a half years that I worked as a manufacturer's representative on a commission basis, I regularly called on one hundred sixty field stores and offices. At each point I endeavored to make friends with every individual involved in selling. This included not only the store managers and field salesman, but the store people as well. I think that I was pretty successful in doing this. On that basis I felt that I had in the vicinity of five hundred people helping me sell my products. These folks were working for me when I was on vacation or perhaps off for a few days because of illness. And, of course, the manufacturer similarly benefitted from this additional sales help.

Another benefit to manufacturers by virtue of having jobbers is that their need for large credit departments is diminished.

Of course, there are a few manufacturers who try to eat their cake and have it, too. They like to have jobbers helping them, but will sell direct when they have the chance. What the customer doesn't realize is that in a lot of these instances he isn't getting the product or service any cheaper. The manufacturer is simply cutting the jobber out of the picture and pocketing the difference!

Also, there are some so-called jobbers who are not worthy of the name. They are telephone and order book brokers who render no real service. They simply skim off some of the cream. They help no one but themselves.

And another thing. the oil field supply business is quite different from other retail businesses. You wouldn't call a groceryman at 2:00 A.M. for some groceries, would you?

But it isn't at all rare for an oil field supply man to be called at that hour, or on Sunday afternoons or on holidays.

Nor is it unusual for a supply man to be asked to deliver material to drilling locations, some quite distant from the store. In some instances the value of the material delivered does not equal that of the gasoline used in delivering it!

Another practice unique to the oil field supply business is that a supply man is often asked to secure materials not normally stocked by the supply stores. I have provided toilet tissue, sheets and other bedding for company bunk

*A Snow Scene in Ohio During the Great Blizzard of 1978.*

houses, razor blades to scrape paint, you just about name it. If you were to go into a clothing store and ask for some tong dies or tool joint compound, you would be told that you were in the wrong store, that you needed to go to an oil field supply store for those items. But not so in the oil field supply business!

The reason that I have gone to some pains in pointing out the above facts, is that because of them the economics of the oil field supply business are different, too. If the supply companies are expected to do all these things in order to keep a drilling rig or lease operating, the customer must be willing to allow them a decent profit on what they sell to them. They just can't survive on the same margin of profit that a supermarket can live with.

## Chapter LXVII

### A SALES MEETING TO REMEMBER

During the thirty-three years that I worked for Republic Supply Company we probably had an average of two sales meetings a year.

I have known people who thought that sales meetings were a waste of time and money. I disagree. Of course, sales meetings will vary a lot, and measuring the value of any individual meeting is relative, kind of like saying: "How old is Mary?" or "How long is a lane?" However, the purpose of this discourse is not to evaluate sales meetings.

I especially recall one sales meeting that I went to. One day, while I was managing Republic's store at New Concord, Ohio, our Executive Vice-President, Mr. J.C. Bergin, called. In something like two weeks he wanted me and our two field salesmen to fly to St. Louis and meet him, another man from the home office and some of the boys from the two stores in Illinois, for a sales meeting.

I called an airline office in Columbus and made reservations for the three of us. On the day we were to make the trip, we drove to Columbus and put our car in long term parking. When we went to the ticket counter we found that the airline's computer was out of order so there was no way that the ticket clerk could find our reservations. But he boarded us anyway.

Now, the two young salesmen had never flown before, and they were a little nervous to start with. It was pretty oldhat to me as I had flown quite a lot before. But just after we had gotten airborne, we began to hear some peculiar, rather weird noises. One of the young men — Wayne Farris — asked me what those noises were. I said that I really didn't know, but that they weren't anything unusual and nothing to be alarmed about, as I had heard them a lot of times before when on other flights. You might say I was telling a white lie of sorts, but I saw no good reason to alarm him.

Then, a little later I went to the restroom. On the way back to my seat I stopped and visited with a fellow passenger. He had gotten on the plane at Pittsburgh. He said: "You know, they're having engine trouble on this plane. In fact, they put a mechanic on at Pittsburgh, and he's monitoring the performance of the engines now." I am not one to get unduly nervous or excited, but I must confess that I was rather glad when we touched down at St. Louis.

I never told Wayne, or the other salesman, Vaughn Ousley, about this. The return flight was on a different plane, in fact a different model altogether, and the flight was smooth as silk.

After we had gotten back home I noticed that I had left my house slippers in the motel in St. Louis where we had stayed. So I called the motel and asked them to send the slippers to me. I told them I would mail them some money to cover the shipping costs. I sent them two or three dollars. But when the package came, I had to pay collect charges. Counting the cost of the phone call, I must have had six or seven dollars tied up in getting my slippers back, so there is some question as to how profitable an operation that was.

## Chapter LXVIII

## AND NOW, 1987

It is now August of 1987. Things are not exactly booming, but they look a lot better than they did a year ago. The first two or three months of this year were still pretty depressed. There were people applying for food stamps and other government assistance who had never found it necessary before.

But since that time there has been a gradual improvement in the outlook in the oil field. Admittedly, it has been slow and there is still no dancing in the streets. But there is optimism now in places where a year ago there was only pessimism.

In July of last year the national rig count was below seven hundred. In the past month it has gone above one thousand. Last year at this time the posted price of West Texas intermediate crude oil was something around $10.00 per barrel. This summer it reached $20.00 per barrel. Right now it seems to have stabilized at $19.00.

During the past year the OPEC countries have met several times and tried to give some stability to the oil market by controlling their production. But the volatile Persian Gulf situation is a thing that keeps us all guessing. The frightening aspect of it all is that by opening or closing of a few valves in the Middle East the price of crude oil can be changed dramatically.

*A Pumping Well in the Old Wheat Field in Loving County near Mentone. The Delaware sand is still producing after sixty years.*

It is almost ridiculous that a superpower like the United States should be at the mercy of a few developing countries, not militarily, but economically. It reminds us of what we were told as a child, that what frightened an elephant the most was not a lion but a mouse.

But our petroleum industry will survive. If it does not, our great country will not. I think it is bad that the several

**157**

regions of our country should be polarized on a matter so vital to our economic and national security as our energy policy. It is neither good for our country that the people in New England should "freeze in the dark" as some have suggested, or that the State of Texas should suffer under a fiscal crisis because of the decline in oil prices. We all need each other.

## Chapter LXIX

## THE RANCHERS

I feel that one section of this book should be devoted to the ranchers. Earlier I mentioned some of these ranchers who were in the Kermit area when I arrived on the scene.

When I came to West Texas I heard a number of stories about the ranchers, how oilmen and people who worked on drilling rigs had been driven from leases at the point of a gun. How utterly difficult the ranchers were to negotiate with. And how, if you had accidentally hit one of their cows or bulls, it would instantly turn out to be a highly valuable, prize animal.

I am in no position to say that these stories are not true. but I can tell you of my own experiences with these people and I can honestly say that they have all been pleasant ones. And I have formed many friendships with ranchers and their families.

If I have heard stories about the mean old ranchers, I have also heard accounts of people with oil companies and drilling contractors who cut the ranchers fences, who shot their livestock and who wantonly and unnecessarily cut up their range land with their trucks. As before, I am in no position to confirm or deny these stories.

One time back in the 1960's, one of our employees was delivering a sub-surface pump to a well on the west end of

*Charles Mitchell and Friend at Ranch House Southeast of Kermit*

Cheyenne Draw, about twelve miles northwest of Kermit. To reach the well it was necessary to cross some of Tom Lineberry's range land. It had snowed and the road was slick. Some of Mr. Lineberry's cattle were along the road. Our driver skidded into one of them, a bull. It had apparently broken a leg.

When our man returned to the store he told me what had happened. I immediately called Mr. Lineberry's ranch foreman and reported it to him.

The next morning I saw Mr. Lineberry in the cafe. I told him that our people would be in touch with his lawyer and do the right thing. He shrugged it off and said that nothing much would come of it. And as far as I know, nothing much did.

These people are, for the most part, pioneer families. When they came to this part of the country, the environment was anything but inviting. It took people of fortitude and courage to face these challenges. They are a proud people. They do not expect the newcomers to treat them with awe, but they do want to be treated as equals.

Earlier in this book I have referred to the late 40's as the "Early years". This word early is a relative one. These years were early to me, but to these pioneer families they were anything but early. They had been in West Texas fifty or more years before I arrived on the scene.

Another thing. While they certainly wouldn't turn down any oil royalties, they want to prove to themselves and to others that they could have made it without the oil. And I think most of them could have done so.

*A Hopper Jack Knife Pulling Unit. Picture taken in the 1960's. Courtesy Longhorn Service and Drilling Company and Sorrells Photo Shop.*

# Chapter LXX

## THE CAPS

I am not a collector of caps per se. But over a period of time I have accumulated something like a couple of dozen of them. Each of them has a sentimental value to me, each represents an individual or organization with whom I have had a pleasant relationship.

In my living room I have a rack for eleven of these caps, immediately above my mantel. The accompanying photo will give you an idea of how they look. Space will not allow an extensive discussion of these or the others that I have but I will give you a brief resume of some of them.

In the center is a Republic Supply Company, Ranger, Texas cap. This has a special sentimental appeal for me, first because I worked for that company for thirty-three years and second because they no longer have a store in Ranger. For that reason it is somewhat of a collector's item as far as I am concerned. The same might be said of the Oilwell cap just to the right of the Republic cap. In the past year that company merged with National Supply and the new entity is known as National-Oilwell.

To the left of center is one from Union Supply Company. I have many friends with that company. These friendships extend back to the 1940's. Next left is Best Oil Field Supply Company, New Concord, Ohio. This has a special appeal to me because it is owned by some good friends of mine, the Lingafelter Family, who were formerly employees of Central Supply Company of Logan, Ohio. Harold D. Miller Trucking Co. is next left. A good personal friend, I am reminded of how impressive an operation Mr. Miller ran. Republic kept a lot of their tubular goods in his pipe yard. His yard was a model of order and efficiency. Last on the left is Hondo Pipe and

Supply Co., who had stores in Roswell and Carlsbad, New Mexico. One day I was in their Roswell store wearing a cap of one of their competitors. Rick Roberts, the manager, took me to task for not wearing his cap. When I got back home I put on one of his caps. Then I went to a cafe and had a picture taken of me and a cute little waitress. I sent the picture to him with this caption: "McWorkman proudly wears his Hondo Pipe and Supply Company cap".

Second right from center is Palmer Pipe and Supply, Inc., founded by Charles Palmer. Many years earlier he was an employee of Republic Supply Company. A good customer of brother Holt's business and later, of mine. Next right is Ira Pump and Supply, a family owned supply store at Ira, Texas. And next right after that, Dunco Oilfield Supply Co., Inc. of Levelland, Texas. This supply company was founded by Peck Williams and his wife, June, and some other associates. Peck was a former employee of Republic Supply Co. and you may recall I

162

made mention of him earlier in this book.

The angle at which these caps hang on the rack suggests that they are in deep thought. Some have suggested that they might be sad, or dejected. But I prefer to believe that they are in a mood of sober contemplation, reflecting upon the many changes that have occurred in the oil field in the last forty years or so. And if I were able to tilt them up a little where they would be facing us more directly, I feel that they would project a positive attitude and one of confidence in the future.

In case the reader has noticed that I have said nothing about the two pictures on the ends, neither of them have anything to do directly with the oil field. The one on the left was given to me by a friend of mine who goes to Laughlin, Nevada, sort of another Las Vegas, from time to time. The name on the cap is Sam's Place. The one on the right was given to me by another friend who had been travelling in the southeastern states, including Kentucky. On the cap it says: "I've Been Horsing Around".

*Two Oilfield Trucks Ready for Action. [Courtesy of D.L. Handlin Trucking Co. and Sorrells Photo Shop]*

**163**

## Chapter LXXI

## THE PEOPLE WHO HAD THE COURAGE TO TRY

I guess that we will have to say that the oilman, particularly the wildcatter, is a gambler. As stated earlier, the success rate for exploratory wells is about sixteen percent or one in six. In the earlier years the odds were hardly that good. Of course, the prospector tries to minimize his risks by making the best possible use of all the available geologic and seismic data. So it isn't exactly like playing a slot machine. But it is still a gamble and it still takes guts!

But from my perspective there are two kinds of gamblers. There are those who derive their gains from the losses of others, from the toss of the dice, a hand in poker or a stock market manipulation. And there are those who have had the courage, the guts if you will, to try to accomplish something with less than cinch odds. And what they do accomplish will add to, not detract from, the wealth available to others. Theirs is a productive kind of gambling.

I think that basically this characterizes most of the people associated with the oil industry. Gamblers perhaps, but I prefer to call them the people who dare to try!

## Chapter LXXII

## AND NOW THE STOCK MARKET PLUNGE

I thought I had seen just about everything in the past eight years.  But I think what happened on Wall Street in October of 1987 deserves a spot in this book.  I realize that it is not directly related to the oil field and I do not own a share of stock myself.  But I am afraid that it will have some impact upon all of us.

The Dow Jones average had been climbing for quite a few months. The way it had been going up was unreal. Many people — myself included — felt that a crash was inevitable.  There was nothing in the economy to justify or support such a bull market.

The Dow peaked at 2722.42 on August 25 of this year. On Friday, October 16, the market closed at 2246.74.  At the close of business on Black Monday, October 19, the Dow stood at 1738.74, a loss of 508.32 points in one day of trading, and a five hundred billion loss in stock value!  It was a 22.6 percentage loss, compared to a loss of 12.8 percent on the first day of the market crash in 1929.

It has rebounded somewhat since that time, but not as much, and certainly not as dramatically as it fell.

At this point in time the event has affected the price of crude oil or the rotary rig count very little.  Let us hope that things continue that way.

## Chapter LXXIII

## ANOTHER SCAM:
## THE LIMITED PARTNERSHIP DRILLING FUNDS

In some earlier chapters I have discussed some forms of larceny that have existed in the oil fields. While perhaps a little more dignified than stealing boards from a lumber yard or pilfering oil from a neighboring lease, some of the Limited Partnership Drilling Programs are no less dishonest. I am not suggesting that all of these programs are not on the up and up. I would recommend caution and if something sounds too good to be true, it probably isn't.

A typical program works like this. In early 1985, the principals set up what they call the 1985 I Drilling Program. Limited Partnerships shares sell at $5,000 each. Some wells are actually drilled and put into production. Along in June or July dividends are issued to the participants. These dividends will run like $600 on a $5,000 share. Also, the shareholders are led to believe that later on in the year there will be another dividend. That's quite a bit better than seven or eight percent on a certificate of deposit isn't it? The participants are so enthused that they buy more shares in 1985 I. Some even borrow money to do so. And, of course, they tell their friends about it. Anything this good should be shared with others.

In the meantime, the shareholders are informed that the 1985 I program is completely subscribed, but that a second program, 1985 II, is being formed with shares, as in the earlier program, being sold at $5,000 each.

While there is some actual drilling activity, the dividends issued to the earlier participants in 1985 I are actually coming from the shares purchased in the latter stages of 1985 I and 1985 II. The participants in 1985 II will probably only get what the little boy shot at.

In effect, the scheme was a glorified form of chain letter. The earlier participants didn't do too bad, but the further you got from that point, the less favorable were your chances. The last ones in on the deal would probably realize no dividends and most likely lose their principal.

What little oil activity takes place is strictly window dressing. In the meantime, the instigators of the scheme are living high on the hog and ratholing a big part of what the last investors in 1985 I and in 1985 II have put into them. The dividends that the investors expected to receive later on in 1985 never materialize.

The eventual result is Chapter 11 Bankruptcy. The instigators are convicted of fraud. But most of the investors have simply lost what they put into the Funds.

*Scene at one of the Permian Basin Oil Shows*

I bought a $5,000 share in one of these programs. I should have known better. I had seen too many of these promoters during the time I was in Ohio. The pictures of the promoters in the literature that was sent me gave me a sense of de-ja vu. I felt that I had seen them, or their ilk, somewhere before and the recollection was tinged with something vaguely unpleasant. Sure, these guys didn't look like tramps, they had to be fairly impressive, but there were those bar room smiles that I had learned not to trust.

I don't know whether or not these fast buck artists share their lists of suckers or not, but I suspect that they do. After the scheme I had invested in had folded, I have had letters and phone calls from people who had investment opportunities to offer. Some of them took the approach that while the Fund I had just invested in had soured, there were some good ones, and maybe I could recoup my losses by getting in on one of them.

Of course, not all of these scams are oil field related. A couple of weeks ago I had a call from a fellow in Sherman Oaks, California. He asked if I was indeed Lee McWorkman and if I still lived at 133 Amelia, in Kermit, Texas. After I had confirmed those facts, he told me of a fabulous investment opportunity that he had to offer. It would pay in the vicinity of thirty-five percent dividends in a matter of two years. He then told me that the shares in this venture were being subscribed at $11,000 each. He asked if this was within the range of my finances. I told him that I would answer his question by saying that I just didn't believe I was interested. He lost no time in hanging up the phone.

And a few days ago a gentleman in Dallas called me and offered me an opportunity to participate in a promising oil well drilling program. Again, I declined with thanks.

And just today, while I was editing my manuscripts, a lady in California called me. What she had to offer was rare coins. She said a profit of eighteen percent per annum was to be had.

Good news sure does travel fast!

## Chapter LXXIV

## THE LAST TIME AROUND

It was my last time around on my itinerary as a travelling salesman. After that I would hang it up for good on my career as a salesman.

It was April of 1984. For the past five and a half years I had been working as a self-employed commission salesman for a manufacturer of oil field equipment. I had enjoyed my work and had made a good living in the process of doing it, but I wanted to do some travelling and also spend more time on writing my books.

This last swing was a little emotional at times. I had called on something like one hundred sixty stores and offices and regularly contacted at least five hundred people. This I had done over a routine of five to six weeks. The people I had seen were more than mere business statistics. They were real, live, beautiful people and I had made friends with just about all of them.

Some of the folks that I would see on this last official trip I would be seeing again from time to time, most certainly those at my home base, Kermit, and also those in Odessa, as I would be having occasion to go there from time to time. But for those on the outer fringes of my territory, like Roswell and Artesia in New Mexico and Levelland and Abilene in Texas, it might be a long time before I saw them again.

At Artesia the people at Union Supply Company had baked a cake in my honor for my last visit with them. One of the ladies who worked there hugged my neck. I thought the other one was going to cry. And it was a little rough saying goodbye to some others of my friends in Snyder and Sundown and Levelland, folks like Bob Burnett with Wilson and Bob O'Dell with Dunco.

I knew I would be missing these contacts with my friends in the weeks and months to come. How many times I had told myself on a Friday at the end of a hard week of driving and making sales calls that I thought it about time to call it quits, and then on the following Monday I could hardly wait to get going again. But I couldn't have it both ways. I would be entering another phase in my life. There is always a certain amount of pain in making such changes. But I would not regret doing it.

As far as I am concerned, there is nothing more precious in this world than friendships. Nor are they a sometime thing. During the thirty-eight and a half years that I was in the business I made many friends among my customers. These people will always be my friends long after we have both retired and there is no longer a business relationship between us. I have known of instances where purchasing agents for companies were the center of attraction — salesmen always wanting to buy their lunch, take them hunting or fishing. Then, after they had retired they would meet their erstwhile friends on the street and they wouldn't even know them.

To me, life is too short. The friendships I have made with my customers are genuine and are not to be terminated by the retirement of either of us. I still like to see them whenever I can.

Through the years I have also made some lasting friendships with a number of my competitors. These friendships, too, are not to be lightly terminated.

## Chapter LXXV

## THE DEATH OF A COMPANY

I think that it is perhaps fitting that this would be the last chapter in the book. I worked for the company for thirty-three years. In that period of time, I learned to love it. It was more than a source of livelihood, it was family. A kindred feeling existed not only between the employees and the company, but between the employees as well.

And then, a few years after I had retired, it happened. First, a merger of our parent corporation, of which we were a wholly owned subsidiary, into a larger corporation. This was followed about a year later by a selloff of our segment of the entity.

Only a couple of years earlier I had visited their home office in Oklahoma City. You might term it a sales call as I had retired from the Company three years earlier and was now representing the Clow Corporation. But it was also a reunion of sorts, too, and I saw a number of the old employees with whom I had worked for many years. They showed me around their nice new offices and gave me a guided tour of their impressive central warehouse, which, with some eighteen wheelers, kept the forty odd field stores stocked with material. How little did I suspect that in less than four years these things would no longer exist and that most of the people I was now seeing would be gone, too. And I guess it is best that I didn't.

While the takeover was not necessarily a hostile one, it was as though we had been invaded by a foreign power. The traditions of the company, the esprit de corps, were a thing of the past. What any of us had done in days gone by was of no interest to the new owners. Indeed, it was as if the company had died.

*A Jack Knife Rotary Drilling Rig. [Courtesy of Pico Drilling Co., Breckenridge, Texas and Sorrells Photo Shop]*

Many of us had been almost literally married to the company. The fact that our fealty and affection were now unrequited was difficult to accept. While it was hard to place the blame on anyone it was almost like discovering that a spouse of many years had become unfaithful.

The case of our company was not an isolated one. In the past few years there have been a number of mergers and takeovers, some friendly, some hostile. Some of them have been smoother than others, with few problems or cost to the employees affected, but most of them have left scars of one form or another.

Some of these marriages of convenience, so to speak, brought out some of the less noble traits in human character: jealousy, bitterness, greed, even revenge. And decisions made under those circumstances were quite often less judicious than those made in a more objective atmosphere. And some of our traditionally accepted rules of ethics and fair play were completely forgotten.

And I can well remember how, in years gone by, how I would counsel the younger employees of our company, and prospective employees, too, about the advantages of working for a large company like ours with a permanence that would extend well beyond my own lifetime. And I believed everything that I said. The fact that what I told them later turned out to be untrue only adds to my sense of loss. I can easily believe that there are other old dyed-in-the-wool, dedicated employees of companies who have had similar experiences.

Should I regret what I said? I think not. You have to believe in something. When you cease to do that, you become a cynic.

*The Winkler County Courthouse. [Courtesy of Bill Beckham and The Winkler County News]*

*Cabot Company's Keystone Carbon Black Plant in Winkler County. After many years in operation the plant was shut down and dismantled in the early 1960's. [Photo courtesy of the Cabot Company and Sorrells Photo Shop]*

*Ralph Lennon, left, Manager of the Artesia Hotel, standing in front of the Hotel with friend. This picture was taken circa 1959. At that point in time it was a gathering place for the oil and gas people in the area. The Hotel held its Grand Opening in November of 1929. It was a six level structure — a basement, four upper floors and a pent house. But twenty-five years later, on October 22, 1976, having been condemned as an unsafe structure, the old landmark was demolished by a wrecking ball and explosives. Many people were saddened by this event.*

*The Moorhead Derrick [Courtesy of Bill Beckham and The Winkler County News]*